To Karen.
From Marianne.

June .1970.

P5
AE

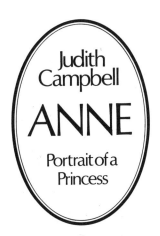

Judith
Campbell

ANNE

Portrait of a
Princess

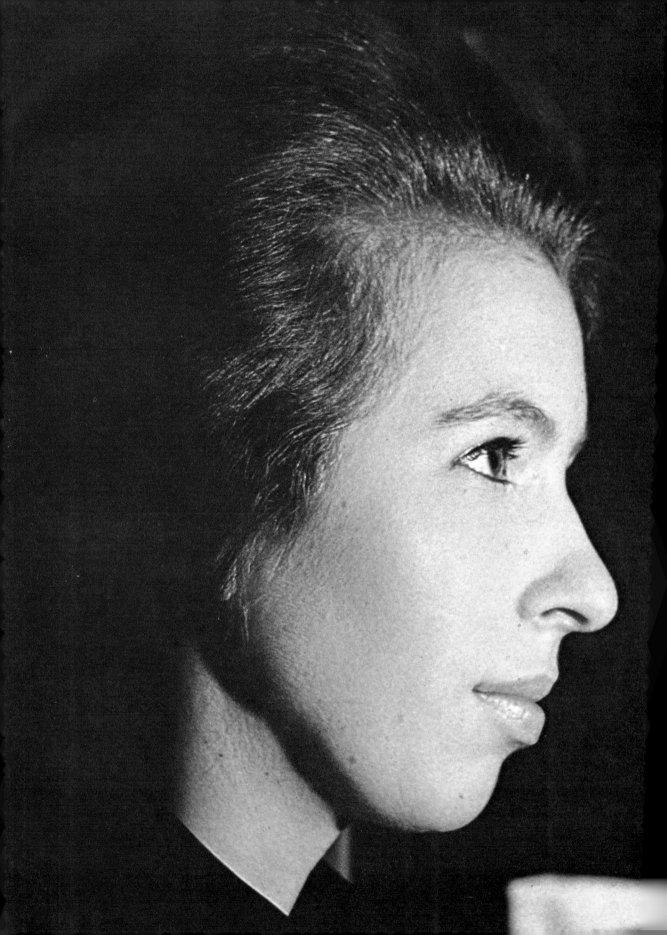

ANNE
Portrait of a Princess

Judith Campbell

Cassell · London

A ROYAL SIGNATURE-WITH-A-DIFFERENCE '(Princess) Anne' adorns the visitors' book of a Church of Scotland Children's Home at Newhaven, Edinburgh.

Royalty normally sign with their first names only but when the Princess wrote the customary 'Anne' at the end of that official visit, there was an indignant protest from the children who had taken over both Her Royal Highness and the day's proceedings. 'But where's your other name?' they demanded. 'You haven't put Princess!'

It was in vain to argue that *Anne* is her name. The children were not to be fobbed off without proof that it really was a Princess who had spent the afternoon with them and in the end she capitulated, adopted a helpful suggestion, and laughingly wrote in the compromise.

This unique signature is in fact the keynote to the Queen's only daughter. Where others might put their job in life as 'Housewife' or 'Managing Director', she has to put 'Princess'. But whereas other people usually have free choice in making such decisions, Anne is a Princess because she was born one.

Her ancestry can be traced in a direct line back to Alfred the Great and William the Conqueror and a thousand years and more of royal power and prestige have gone into the making of the Princess's role.

Prestige and an element of mystery remain but the original concept of royal power has been transmuted down the years into the Royal Family's strong sense of public duty. Others can make suggestions and offer advice as to the ways in which Princess Anne can serve but what she makes of her particular situation in life is, essentially, up to her alone. It is not an easy job,

and must often run contrary to private inclinations and ambitions. In this day and age no one, certainly not the Princess herself, is quite certain what it should entail, where to start, and how best to serve.

The Princess Anne Elizabeth Alice Louise, now fourth in succession and second Lady in the Land, was born just before midday on Tuesday, 15 August 1950, the official announcement of her birth celebrated with a salute fired in Hyde Park by the King's Troop, Royal Horse Artillery; by flags flying, and by the clash and clamour of church bells. She weighed 6 lb., was strong and healthy, and took her place in the family between a brother older by twenty-one months and two younger brothers yet to come.

George VI, third sovereign of the House of Windsor and the Princess's grandfather, was on the throne. Her mother, Princess Elizabeth, then aged twenty-four, was Heir Presumptive. Her father, H.R.H. Prince Philip, Duke of Edinburgh, was a serving officer in the British Navy, in command of H.M. Frigate *Magpie*. Her brother Charles was the future Prince of Wales, and likely one day to become King of England.

Prince Philip registered his daughter's birth in the sub-district of Westminster North-East, and received her ration book and identity card, those now almost forgotten relics of World War II. The baby was about a month old when she made her début in front of an official photographer, and the Press first caught up with her soon afterwards—as she was being carried aboard the train for Scotland and Balmoral, at the start of a journey that was to become a familiar part of her life.

There were more official photographs on 21 October of that year when Princess Anne, wearing a priceless family robe, was christened by the Archbishop of York in the Music Room at Buckingham Palace—her sponsors the Queen (now the Queen Mother), Princess Andrew of Greece (Prince Philip's mother), Princess Margarita of Hohenlohe-Langenburg, Earl Mountbatten and the Hon. Andrew Elphinstone. It is said that she behaved impeccably throughout the ceremony, a precept not always followed in the immediate years to come!

Until she was nearly two, Princess Anne lived with her parents and brother at Clarence House, which faces St James's Park and was the residence of a former Duke of Edinburgh.

In the pleasant nurseries designed for them by Princess Elizabeth and Prince Philip, and looked after by their Nannie, Mrs (a courtesy title) Lightbody, assisted by Miss Anderson—who later took charge—the children lived a happy and normal existence. Maybe the nursery routine was more formal than the easier-going system that later evolved, but the emphasis on manners, on being tidy, clean and correct, was 'just life', and it never occurred to Princess Anne or her brother that a higher nursery standard might be expected of them, or that they were in any way different from other children. In fact the pattern probably deviated little from that of the majority of nurseries in well-to-do families of the time. Going to see 'Granpa and Grannie' meant visiting the King and Queen at one of the royal residences. There was always an unobtrusive detective to accompany the 'pushing out' in St James's or Green Park—occasions that became unnecessary on the move to Buckingham Palace with its big acreage of gardens—and a quick get-away to be made at the first hint of a crowd. From the earliest age the royal children are taught to wave back at people when travelling by car, a friendly gesture that appears perfectly natural until you realize that other people do not normally do this. But by and large the most outstanding aspect of the early life of all the children is that it is chiefly unremarkable. The Queen and Prince Philip have done their utmost to see that this should be so. They have made it a deliberate policy to keep their children out of the limelight for as long as possible, but no parents could be more relaxed, or more fun, in their children's company. The Royal Family's private life has a gay informality about it, laced with a 'goonish' sense of humour that is the perfect antidote to the strain of a public life of official duties.

In the autumn of 1951 Princess Elizabeth and Prince Philip returned from travelling thousands of miles over the length and breadth of Canada, to find the King making apparently steady progress after a recent, serious operation. His Majesty was well enough to enjoy a family Christmas at

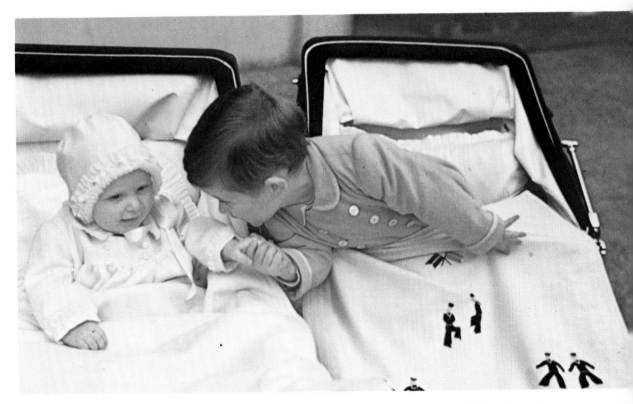

Sandringham that year, and Prince Charles and Princess Anne accompanied their parents to the reunion. On 31 January 1952, Princess Elizabeth and Prince Philip set off on another extended tour to cover Kenya, Ceylon, Australia and New Zealand but returned suddenly on 7 February after receiving the sad news that King George VI had died peacefully in his sleep.

On the death of her father, Princess Elizabeth became Queen and Prince Charles, Heir Apparent. These were momentous events that obviously affected the whole family, and although Princess Anne was only a baby at the time, both were to have a bearing not only on her future life but on her personality.

The move to Buckingham Palace was not long delayed. A nursery wing was quickly adapted from rooms first used by the children's mother and aunt as young girls, and then as Princess Margaret's private suite before she and the Queen Mother transferred to Clarence House. And here, in these high-ceilinged day and night nurseries and in the adjoining schoolroom, all now taken over by Prince Edward, Princess Anne spent much of her childhood, until she was thirteen and went to boarding school.

The nurseries are not much changed from those days. The day nursery walls are still painted eau-de-nil. The big display cabinet with its delicate china contents that Queen Mary gave her grand-daughter Princess Elizabeth stands in the same place above the cupboard housing the modest collection of toys, many of them handed down to the younger boys by their elder brother and

sister. Princess Anne's cabinet, also given by Queen Mary, now lacks a few favourite ornaments that the Princess took to her own room at the front of the Palace. Today the nursery sofa and two easy chairs are upholstered to match the original glazed chintz curtains, the pair of South American lovebirds are no more and Prince Charles's corgi died in 1968. But the Princess's Sherry, a lop-eared version of the same breed, remains as much a part of the nursery scene as when the dog's owner used to sprawl on her tummy in front of the TV set, to watch her favourite cowboy films.

All the children have shared a bedroom with their Nannie longer than is usual, but this is chiefly because, despite the vast size of Buckingham Palace, the only possible bedrooms, once away from the nursery wing, are far off down the corridor. Prince Charles migrated first, followed, on the birth of Prince Edward, by Princess Anne, who has a bedroom on the other side of their shared sitting-room.

Today Prince Edward, long promoted to the attractive wooden bed that was specially designed and presented to Prince Charles, sleeps with Miss Anderson in the night nursery, where Princess Anne had her cot in Mrs Lightbody's day. In the school holidays Prince Andrew now has the room leading off, which Miss Anderson shared in turn with the older children. When Princess Anne moved out she took a prized possession with her, the bed given her by her mother, which the Queen used on board the *Gothic* when she and Prince Philip toured the world in 1953. One love that was left behind was Bugs Bunny, a dilapidated toy rabbit in a pink dress, which the Princess bequeathed to Miss Anderson 'to keep her company'.

Some of the official photographs taken of Princess Anne as a small girl show her with a doll's pram and occupant—the playthings that by tradition all little girls are supposed to prefer. But the Queen is not alone in recalling her small daughter as more boyish than girlish in her tastes, and however much anyone tried to interest the Princess in dolls, she never played with them. The doll's pram, still stored in the nursery 'luggage room', is in unnaturally mint condition, the doll inside showing no signs of wear and tear, and without even the consideration of a name.

With her fair curls, blue eyes and pink and white complexion, it was inevitable that the Princess's public image as a small girl should be that of the gentle, fairy-tale princess. She was an enchanting child to dress, and to some extent took a feminine pleasure in wearing the frilly dresses and fur- or flower-trimmed bonnets expected of the Queen's little daughter on special occasions. But it is not chance that photographs of the time show her at her happiest in the Queen's choice of holiday clothes—jerseys, and the slacks that were the forerunners of the Princess's cherished teenage jeans.

The truth is that where many little girls dream of being a princess, this particular Princess dreamed of being a boy. As she grew older the dream changed somewhat, although she remains a bit of a tomboy even today. Reading books of olden times made her think it would have been fun to live in those days, and she liked to imagine herself as some simple country wench of the first Elizabethan era.

From the earliest age Princess Anne liked to use her brain and fingers on jig-saw puzzles, on modelling with Plasticine or cutting out favourite Christmas cards to paste in an album. When at Windsor she and Prince Charles enjoyed playing in the grounds of Royal Lodge with Y Bwthyn Bach, the miniature thatched cottage given to the Queen as a child by the people of Wales. But her abiding loves were the rocking horse that also once belonged to the Queen and Prince Charles's toy wooden trap with rakish trotting pony, which she spent hours pedalling up and down the corridor outside the nursery.

This gay, affectionate, lively little girl was overflowing with energy, and liked to be actively engaged in the heart of things. Always quick off the mark and never missing a single trick, she was, and remains, very much her father's daughter. But as Prince Philip rightly contends, there are so many factors that go into the making of someone's personality. Being a girl, and second in the family to a brother who was not only older by nearly two years but also the heir to the throne, subconsciously made her feel of less importance. Their parents made no difference between the two children, and if the Princess has always been rather more moody than the boys, the Queen remembers her as a very easy little girl. Nevertheless, for a time and when far too young consciously to register her emotions, Prince Philip thinks his daughter perhaps felt herself somewhat neglected.

She was always adventurous—Princess Anne insists that it was she who climbed the trees while Prince Charles looked on—and needed no urging to join her brother on an expedition when they 'trooped over the roof' at Windsor Castle. The exploit was not a very popular one, but it was repeated only a year or so back when they took a friend to look at the clock on the tower. On this occasion the two big bells on the roof which have hammers that can be worked from the outside proved irresistible, and the mounting of the Guard far below at a little before midday was enlivened by twenty-four chimes ringing out at different times for no particular reason.

Princess Anne has always been very brave, and the urge to keep up with an older brother and do

everything he did produced a veneer of apparent toughness. As a child this adventurous, 'try anything once' spirit was extended even to food. She was obligingly ready to taste new dishes, if never backward in condemning those that did not appeal—including the peas that still remain one of the few things she will not eat.

She was only a baby when she was brought to the door to see her parents off on a foreign tour. Far too young to understand that her mother was going away she yet screamed her disapproval of the general commotion and at not being allowed into the royal car—a situation that Prince Charles at the same age would have solemnly accepted. Prince Charles and his sister are very different in character. Even as a small boy he was always a far more 'certain starter' in public, with a built-in instinct for what was required of him.

In the everyday life of the nursery it was Princess Anne who was the unpredictable one, capable of throwing tempestuous if short-lived scenes when thwarted, but also a sweet child, often disarmingly ready, as she still is today, to acknowledge her own misdemeanours.

Accustomed from toddler days to the constant stream of visitors that converges on Buckingham Palace and Windsor Castle, it was natural for her to be friendly towards grown-ups, but she confesses to having disliked small girls on principle, and to having fought with the boys, and considers she 'wasn't actually a very popular person'! Certainly her subconscious feeling of not attracting sufficient attention, combined with a strong, innate bent for leadership that developed at times into 'bossiness', caused plenty of friction between brother and sister. Even today Prince Charles and Princess Anne often do not see eye to eye, and their tastes are very different, but they much enjoy each other's company and take great pleasure in a common wave-length of humour—a sometimes near-fatal bond at public functions. They may still argue a lot, but as Prince Charles says, one of the things about families is that the members still need to go on living with one another, so that arguments have to be forgotten almost as they come to an end.

From the start the Queen and Prince Philip were determined that their children should not be spoiled. Only one or two of the lovely toys presented for the children on Royal Tours and other occasions were handed over. Some of the remainder were kept downstairs for use later on, or put on show with others, or sent to children in hospital. The nursery toy cupboard has never therefore been overstocked. Many of the dresses the Princess wore as a tiny baby were handed down from the beautiful white layette presented to the Queen for Prince Charles, and all her everyday childhood clothes were very simple. When Princess Anne went to a Guide camp her equipment was never better, and often less complete than that of the other girls; once when she joined in a swimming gala with them in the Palace swimming-bath, her towel was so disproportionately small that another had to be sent for. It was the same with her clothes and possessions at school; there was nothing to make them stand out from those belonging to other people. This is an outlook the Princess has

carried into adult life. Even when she was older and first went to the stables where she and her horses still further her riding and Eventing ambitions, the 'tack' with which Princess Anne arrived was very inadequate compared with that of the usual well-off client, and was only supplemented by degrees.

Good manners, obedience and consideration for others were insisted on whether they were in the nursery or with their parents, but otherwise the children have been brought up with as much freedom as possible, and with a great deal of fun and laughter. As a small child Princess Anne, like her brothers, had her share of deserved nursery spankings, given and taken without rancour. To be sent out of the room was the most favoured, if least minded punishment, but being deprived of a favourite TV programme was the one the Princess most disliked.

Considering the overflowing official and social programmes that the Queen has to fulfil each year, it is astonishing that she manages to see as much of her children as she does. State Visits, or a Commonwealth Tour like that of 1953, may bring a separation of some months, but otherwise school vacations are kept by both parents, whenever possible, for the children. Prince Philip's varied work and interests frequently take him abroad, but he tries to arrange it so that he can spend all, or most of the holidays with his family. Until Prince Charles and Princess Anne left school and were there more often to see for themselves something of their father's exceptionally busy life, Prince Philip sometimes thought that his children imagined he spent his entire existence in the manner of the carefree weeks of leisure at Balmoral!

With all their essential activities, it is scarcely surprising that when the Queen and Prince Philip are in London, the younger children have to keep to a daily routine for seeing their parents. Now that Prince Charles and Princess Anne are grown up they are at Buckingham Palace more than ever before, but like most young people of their age they are busy with their own lives and their parents see relatively little of them after they have been in to say 'Good morning'.

Like all the children Princess Anne went down-stairs to see her parents after breakfast and before lessons—a custom prolonged until she went to boarding school in 1963. The period from after tea until bed-time has always belonged to the younger ones, with the Queen and Prince Philip following them up to the night-nursery to say 'good night' and read a story. The Princess and her brothers also enjoyed the occasional bonus that Prince Edward gets today, that of popping in on the Queen, if she is alone, to say 'hullo' en route for the garden after lunch, or of finding their mother somewhere in the grounds spending a few spare minutes in exercising the dogs.

The holidays in Norfolk and Scotland are almost entirely given over to the children. When in London the weekends are habitually spent at Windsor, and here again the children are with their parents for most of the time, including family lunch on Sundays directly they are old enough, and if there is not a large house-party.

THE QUEEN DID NOT GO AWAY TO school, and Princess Anne is the first British Sovereign's daughter to break from the tradition of entirely home education, undertaken by tutors and governesses. Before going into the Navy, Prince Philip had the experience of both preparatory and public school, and obviously this weighed heavily in the decision to send his sons to boarding school, although in these times there could really be no other conclusion. In Princess Anne's case it was not quite so simple.

Where family tradition favours it, the subject of boarding school for girls is anyway more complicated than in the case of boys, and with royalty even a day school produces problems not usually encountered by ordinary people. The difficulties of security, publicity and the Press loom large, and these are points that can affect the school, staff and other children, as well as the pupil in question.

Princess Anne's formal education began in the traditional royal manner in the autumn of 1955, when at the age of five she started lessons with Miss Peebles, Prince Charles's governess, who came to the Palace from the household of the late Princess Marina, Duchess of Kent. The question of class-mates was solved in May 1957 when two little girls of the Princess's own age, Caroline Hamilton, eldest grand-daughter of the Dean of Windsor, and Susan Babington-Smith, started coming daily to share her lessons. Although Prince Charles went to day school before going on to preparatory school, the idea of his sister also going to one was not seriously entertained, and Miss Peebles's regime continued until the Princess was thirteen.

Miss Peebles was excellent with young children, catching their interest by weaving many of their lessons around the notable people, happenings and places in any way connected with the Palace and the Constitution, and Princess Anne's own life. She also continued the policy begun with Prince Charles of taking her young pupils out and about London, outings that began with such items as the Zoo, St Paul's Cathedral, and suitable exhibitions like that of 'Toys through the Ages', which the Princess enjoyed when she was seven. Since the Queen's seasonal visits to her country estates tally almost exactly with the school holidays, the Princess would have had little chance, without these expeditions, which were expanded as the children grew older, of getting to know London until she left school altogether.

The lessons with Miss Peebles were later augmented at different times by various outside tutors, although it was sometimes a problem, even in London, to find this source of extra education. Additional history was included in this way in the summer of 1962, and Princess Anne also started Latin lessons with a tutor in that same November.

To speak French fluently is essential for royalty. In 1957 Mademoiselle Bibiane de Roujoux arrived in Scotland for a month for French conversation with Prince Charles and his sister. Two years later the Queen and Prince Philip arranged for Lieut. Jean Lajeunesse, a young French-Canadian they met in Canada, to come to Balmoral and supplement the French lessons given to the Palace class during the previous term by a teacher from the Lycée in Kensington.

When the Princess was eleven, she and her class-mates began general lessons in French, the study of pictures and other cultural subjects, with Mrs Untermeyer—a friend of the Queen's who had taught her and Princess Margaret French during the war. And in 1962 Mrs Untermeyer took Princess Anne and her own niece to stay with the Marquis de St Genys in the Loire Valley for a fortnight's French tuition.

Instruction in French continued all through the years at Benenden, but on leaving school the Princess was the first to admit that the language still did not trip easily from her tongue. In the autumn of 1968, with schooldays just behind her, she decided to take a course in French, and with characteristic 'do or die' thinking opted for the 'crash' curriculum. Six weeks of constant French, working five days a week from 9 a.m. to 6.45 p.m., enabled the Princess to appreciate the finer points of Jean-Louis Barrault's production of *Rabelais* at the Old Vic in September 1969. It also convinced her that, though 'endless courses until Doomsday' may well be included in her lot, none of them shall be quite as tough as that first one!

When Prince Charles first started school, and during the years until she followed suit, Princess Anne may well have felt that once again she was being left out, and how much better it would have been to be a boy. Fond as she was of her governess, it yet irked her independent spirit to know there was someone in the house who always knew exactly where she was and what she was doing. Before sampling the comparative 'outside' freedom of boarding school, the Princess could not consciously be aware of limitations that had always been a normal part of life, but the years between about eleven and fourteen were not always easy. Unlike Prince Charles, she did not seem to need the self-assurance gained from companionship with others, but presented a self-contained, self-confident air to the world, with an underlying reticence that hid hurts and dissatisfactions beneath an apparently tough façade.

Like Prince Philip, whose school reports regularly contained the comment 'Could do better if he tried harder!', Princess Anne's outlook is not that of a scholar. But she has a high intelligence and interest in all she does, and appreciates her brain being 'stretched' to capacity. By the time she was twelve she felt that she had outgrown lessons at home, and that it would be better for her to get out and see an entirely different circle of people and gain a wider education.

When asked if she wanted to go to school, the Princess's answer was 'yes', although she candidly admits that the outcome would probably have been the same had she said 'no'.

The Queen and Prince Philip had in fact decided that there was really no alternative to boarding school. The question of suitable tutors was becoming more acute, and the Queen had come to feel that for Princess Anne a complete education at home would not have helped her later on in life, although she is not certain that boarding school was the perfect answer.

Various factors influenced the choice of school: the standard and class of education in relation to the modern royal outlook; the type of girls who went there, and whether they were likely to accept the Princess on her own merits rather than be influenced unduly by her position; and the games and outdoor activities included, which were likely to be important to the new pupil. The school had to be within reasonable reach of London and set in sufficient grounds of its own to ensure privacy.

The final choice was Benenden School, an independent school for girls that stands in a large park on the outskirts of the Kentish village of Benenden, 380 feet above sea-level on one of the higher points of the Weald. The large, handsome old house was built by the first Earl of Cranbrook in 1862 and modernized by Viscount Rothermere in 1912. It became a school twelve years later and has since been extended at different times by the addition of two 'out' houses and various blocks of class-rooms and music rooms.

Miss E. B. Clarke, the Headmistress, is a Master

of Arts and Bachelor of Literature (Oxon), in addition to being a Justice of the Peace and someone who is more than wise in the ways and needs of generations of schoolgirls. The school is divided into six Houses of about fifty-four girls each, under the overall charge of a Housemistress who is also a member of the large and impressively well qualified teaching staff.

Princess Anne went to Benenden at the start of the autumn term in September 1963. She arrived, accompanied by the Queen, after an overnight journey down from Scotland, to begin a way of life that was to occupy most of the next five years, and of which she then knew nothing.

Arrival at a new school is in itself a big ordeal for anyone. On this occasion all 320 or so girls were assembled outside the entrance of the main building to greet the Queen. Half a dozen press men were well in evidence, and the proceedings concluded with Princess Anne being introduced to all the staff—an arduous public trial of anyone's savoir-faire, let alone that of a new girl aged just thirteen. But early training and her own ability to 'rise to the occasion' saw her through—to the welcome moment when she and the Queen were taken 'behind scenes' along corridors cluttered with all the unfamiliar paraphernalia of a beginning of term . . . school trunks and laundry baskets and crowds of girls, laughing and chattering, engrossed in the notice-board, with the occasional tearful newcomer clinging tightly to her mother.

Benenden has a reputation for being very kind to new girls, and an excellent custom of allocating to each one a House Mother, responsible for helping the new arrival find her feet, a practice that in Princess Anne's case proved especially helpful in making first friends. All through her school life the girls at Benenden were very sensible and most co-operative in accepting her as 'just another girl', but at the beginning there was bound to be a slight natural hanging back to offset any suggestion of 'sucking up'. The Princess's House Mother was of the same level in the school

as her protégée, but of one term's standing, and had already linked up with a group of four other friends. The Princess says she 'just sort of tagged along with her . . . they didn't seem to mind' . . . and she was lucky enough to find a group of people who fraternized and were extremely kind to her. At the same time they were 'a caustic lot who knew exactly what they thought about other people, and saved one a lot of embarrassment'.

For somebody who had never been to school before, the Princess seemed remarkably competent, and adept at assessing, and adopting, the best parts from the great deal of advice meted out to all newcomers. Benenden is a large place and it is not easy for the uninitiated to find her way around, but Princess Anne seemed always to arrive from her House in the right form or practice room at the correct time, failed to get either herself or her possessions in half such a muddle as many who had been to school before, and appeared to settle down very quickly.

She cannot remember feeling actually homesick, but, used after Prince Charles went to school to a life in which she was either on her own or with one or two companions, she found, both then and at the beginning of each term, that 'the amount of people and the noise was staggering . . .' It was a side of school life to which she never became fully accustomed, and the Queen thinks that Princess Anne's biggest trial when she went away to school was always being in a crowd and never by herself. Combined with the constant chattering and ringing of bells, it must have been very difficult for someone who liked her own company. And Princess Anne does enjoy her own company, seeking the solitude she can find out alone with a horse in the environs of Windsor, Sandringham or Balmoral, and needing to be solitary at times, as does the Queen.

Apart from this drawback, and that lessened as each term wore on, the Princess thoroughly enjoyed her years at school. To some girls school represents a loss of liberty that they resent, but to Princess Anne Benenden provided a freedom she had never known before, the freedom to be herself, a teenage girl who was just one in a crowd of others. The discipline did not irk her—she considers it an essential when one is young in order to learn to control oneself—but she was certainly no saint. She was noisy and could be as casual as any girl of her age, and her inherent good manners occasionally lapsed. Early training made it entirely natural for her to cope suitably with some out-of-the-ordinary happening, yet an incongruous shyness could make it difficult for her to say 'Good morning' to members of the staff met unexpectedly along the passages. Tidy by nature, it irritated her when others left their chores undone, and although she felt she was being a bit of a 'sucker for punishment' she did sometimes clear up for other people. Yet equally there were days when she felt, 'too bad—if they're going to leave it, then so am I!'

The Princess was in fact a thoroughly normal, happy girl, full of energy and interest, and able to relax and be natural amongst people who never made her feel that she was different, or even allowed themselves to think she should be treated differently. She could be and was occasionally difficult. By the time she reached Upper Fifth she was showing many of the usual signs of girls of that age—becoming a part of that élite clique common in most schools, who are inclined to be full of themselves, quite sure they know best, resentful of being 'ticked off', and engrossed with a youthful, commendable and immense sense of justice and injustice. This stage developed with the Princess, as it does with the majority, into a genuine ability to take responsibility.

All through her school life, without ever being in the smallest degree self-conscious about her position, the Princess showed that instinctive sense of fitness, the wish to keep out of any situation inappropriate to herself, that has been the yard-stick of most of her actions. There have been many times when she would have liked to throw her cap over some specific windmill, and

occasionally she does, but allied to the deep love all their children have for the Queen and Prince Philip is an innate respect for the difficult task their parents have undertaken. The Princess would never consciously embarrass either by 'making a fool of herself' and so inadvertently perhaps making them look foolish.

It was suggested in the Press when Princess Anne first went to Benenden that there would be restrictions put on her choice of friends, but nothing could have been further from the truth. Her parents' dearest wish was that their daughter should be absorbed into the everyday life of the school, and she was absolutely free to make friends how and where she liked. Once the first ice was broken there was certainly no difficulty about this. Apparently a 'natural' for fitting into community life, her gaiety and genuine interest in people and all that goes on, combined with the fundamental honesty of thought and word that is so much a part of her character, made the Princess well liked by both her contemporaries and the staff, and brought her many true friends.

No rules were ever 'bent' for the Princess's benefit. There were no extra outings, no difference in possessions, and nothing ever to set her apart from the rest, with one exception. It is an accepted and necessary part of royal life to have a personal detective. The Queen sometimes feels that, though this is something of which she herself is never even conscious, it might make a difference to Princess Anne's much more independent existence. But in fact she too is entirely accustomed to the presence of the tactful, friendly men who have been in the background of her life ever since she can remember. Whether the Princess drives herself or has a chauffeur, goes shopping, attends public functions or has a social evening out, somewhere around is her detective—not lurking on her heels, but unobtrusively within range in case of need.

Once at the Benenden Riding Establishment her detective was watching while his charge rode inoffensively around the field when his presence caught the attention of some men unloading chairs for the Riding School's annual Open Day. They beckoned the Princess over. 'What's that man watching you for?' demanded one. 'You royalty, or something?'

Princess Anne could scarcely deny the charge, especially since her detective, leaning against the indoor school smoking his pipe, at that moment so obviously *could* only be a policeman! But it was embarrassing when her inquisitor, having followed up the attack with, 'Well, who are you then?' utterly refused to believe her when she told him!

In the early days a photographer with a telescopic lens was discovered by the top gate, and the occasional one optimistically turned up at the riding school, but these were mostly free-lances. The journalists from the national Press seldom

appeared in person unless there was some big occasion, but restricted their interest to inter-mittent telephone calls—ringing up to ask all sorts of questions at odd times, in one instance waking the Headmistress at the unpopular hour of 1.30 a.m.

Ask Princess Anne what she liked doing best academically and she exclaims in horrified tones, 'My goodness, I haven't got a favourite subject!'

In fact she feels she is not good at concentrating on one particular thing for too long, but if she had any pet school subjects then they were history and the geography that she enjoyed particularly at advanced level, finding that the latter subject covered a very wide field, with a great deal of human interest. Maths she considered almost totally beyond her, and neither could she cope with chemistry, but she would have liked to include the physics that appealed to her inquiring and logical

mind. She showed an innate talent for reading aloud, with a sensitive appreciation of the meaning and beauty of poetry—even when under the embarrassing and nervous strain of reciting as a punishment.

The Princess takes pleasure in a 'good write every now and then', such as her vivid description of her feelings when sailing, although English, as a subject, never interested her. She reckoned the grammar was 'way beyond' her and was not particularly inspired by the choice of books in literature classes. Her leisure reading at school was mostly confined to books discovered lying around, whatever the kind providing they were a complete change from work and the school environment.

Intrinsically a 'doer' rather than a long-term 'planner', Princess Anne always appeared to prefer the actual lessons to the necessary 'prep', and compositions written in a literary manner did not come easily. With her shrewd mind and capacity for picking on the salient point, she yet tended to put down the gist without enough facts to back up her arguments, so that her essays did not always do credit to her considerable ability. Princess Anne is also inclined to write as she talks, in a natural colloquial idiom, using the terms of her own generation seasoned with more old-fashioned expressions that add an unexpected and charming piquancy to her conversation. This is one of the reasons why she always writes her own speeches, embodying her normal casual delivery, finding this the most explicit method of putting over what she means. She is sure any speech would sound unconvincing, both in content and delivery, if inspired by anyone else, and although she could, she supposes, be 'fearfully pompous and very sort of correct about it', she does not think anybody would believe a word she said.

The Press for a long time tended rather to belittle Prince Charles's and his sister's intellectual achievements, but this slant had to be altered quickly in view of the Prince's accomplishments

at university, and was also unfair to the Princess. She is very intelligent, with an adaptable, astute mind, and quick to come to grips with the many subjects that interest her. She confesses to being lazy, interpreted by her Headmistress as possessing far more academic ability than she cared to exercise, and working at school only as hard as was strictly necessary! Exams did not bother her unduly, and despite a daunting public concern with the results, she was not worried by her 'O' levels, obtaining six with quite reasonable grades at the first attempt.

The school was optimistic over Princess Anne's prospects for her 'A' levels, and there was natural disappointment all round when she only obtained two of moderate grades. But it is just not true to say that the Princess could not have gone to university if she had wished to. She had the same qualifications as the considerable number of people who go with only two 'A' level subjects, and in addition obtained the Merit in history that is possible for only fifteen per cent of those taking a particular subject. She also passed the Use of English Examination, one that is separate from 'O' or 'A' level, but a requisite for Oxford or Cambridge.

If Princess Anne had gone on to higher education anywhere in Britain, it would have been to one of the new universities, but although the idea was seriously considered it was dropped for a variety of reasons. The Queen thinks that her daughter now appreciates that it is always good to go on adding to one's knowledge, although for one of the Princess's lively temperament courses, even in London, are not easy to fit in. But Her Majesty is not sure how much university life would have helped in the long run, at any rate at that time.

Prince Philip sees the parents' role as trying to encourage their children to do something that might stand them in good stead in the future. He deprecates the modern tendency to live just for the day, but realizes it is difficult to get across to the young that they have got to write themselves some sort of record in life, something to look

back on. The Duke would like to see the Princess gain some kind of solid achievement, but the difficulty is to know what. He is not sure that her riding ambitions, even if she reached the highest level, quite fit the bill, and considers that, in his daughter's case, going to university and getting a degree would not do so either.

As for Princess Anne, basically she does not like the curricula at British universities, and feels her distaste for concentrating on one thing for long would not have eased matters. She also thinks that although university is right for those with the correct academic approach, too many students go there as a means of opting out from doing anything else.

By and large, the chief reason for the Princess not going to university is that she is fundamentally an outdoor type. Her intelligence draws her to the wisdom and knowledge that lie with books and study, but her instincts and interests are in the open air.

The games at school were an obvious joy. Although she did not appreciate netball as much as lacrosse, both provided welcome exercise after sitting at a desk (even if it meant going out into the worst of weather) and the Princess has inherited Prince Philip's games' sense and good eye for a ball. She was in her House First Lacrosse XII for two seasons, and played in the Second School Team in her last year. She was included amongst those who went to the Schools' Lacrosse Tournament in 1968 to help win her section— and scored the personal triumph of remaining unrecognized throughout.

As for tennis, the tuition she received from a Wimbledon coach, Dan Maskell, on the Palace court just before she was nine inspired a game that was good for one of her age. She enjoyed tennis at school and ended up in her House First Team, but insists she 'kind of fell to pieces' directly the play became too serious.

Benenden broadly followed the pattern of days at most boarding schools. A first getting-up bell at seven, with breakfast at 7.40 followed by

a 'breather' for those who, like the Princess, were housed in the main building—even if, unlike her, the majority were not so keen on this run down the drive and back in the chilly hours of early morning. Bed-making came after breakfast, and although the Queen regrets her daughter's lack of interest in the domestic arts, the Princess did not take exception to this chore at school. She found it 'sort of worked off one's breakfast', and certainly learned how to make it quickly!

The school register was taken before prayers at 8.50 a.m., with form work, practices and 'prep' occupying the rest of the morning to 12.50 p.m., with a twenty-minute break in the middle. Games took up part of each afternoon, with the remainder as welcome 'free time', followed by more work from 4.40 p.m. until 7.10 p.m.

Princess Anne always had a very full timetable. At one stage she was learning the oboe in addition

... and a public view

to the piano, but dropped the wind instrument when she did not seem to progress beyond the initial difficulties. Pottery extended the pleasurable use of her hands that began with Plasticine in the nursery, and provided, in the early years, an artistic relaxation she enjoyed. She was a star member of the Dancing Club, always ready to have a go at anything, but making a speciality of Scottish Dancing. She also sang in the school choir. And while not aspiring to quite the same acting ability as her brother, the Princess was in demand for parts in House Dramatic Competitions, particularly for any role requiring clowning, or one of the many dialects that come easily to her tongue.

Occasionally Princess Anne took the part of a man, and that of an outrider in the school pageant was a 'natural' for her. In her last year, partly because she was a choir member, she portrayed

the drunken sailor in the school production of Purcell's *Dido and Aeneas*.

As the Princess worked her way up the school, her quick perception of things that required doing, not necessarily either dramatic or vastly important ones, became more apparent. If there was something to be done, then usually she would notice the fact and do it, without waiting to be asked. She became a House Monitor and eventually Captain of House, equivalent to Deputy Head, a position that developed her authoritative but pleasant way of giving orders. People would do what she wanted quite easily, especially since her ready sense of humour was seldom absent.

Maybe the best comment on Princess Anne's schooldays is that she spent two terms as a member of the Upper Sixth, an honour that is not appointed by authority, but bestowed by the election of the school.

APART FROM THE SCHOLASTIC AND games side of her education, Princess Anne from an early age took part in various activities that helped to develop and widen her interests.

Into this category came the Girl Guides. Like the Queen, the Princess enjoyed her years as a Guide. After an apprenticeship in the Brownie Pack, originally started for Princess Margaret before the war, she was enrolled in the 1st Buckingham Palace Company in 1961, and remained with them until she went to boarding school.

Her fellow Guides came, intact as a Company, from the 12th Westminster. They were a cheerful crew who might call a spade a spade or equally might define it as something considerably less polite. Friendly and direct, they were neither overawed by the identity of their new companion nor by meeting once a week in the summer house in the Palace gardens, or, during winter, in the huge room in the Palace used as a cinema. If they reckoned that P.A., as they called her, was behaving foolishly they said so, and in turn accepted that she herself has seldom suffered fools gladly. They judged people on merit, and when after a comparatively short while her natural bent for leadership became obvious, the Guides themselves voted the Princess into positions of responsibility.

Those years were not all spent lighting bonfires with one match in the Palace shrubbery, learning first aid and how to apply the kiss of life to a repellent rubber dummy, or excelling at knots that came easily to one conversant with boats and ponies. The Company put on two shows in the Palace Throne Room: a Nativity mime in which Princess Anne played the part of Joseph—and was terrified 'on the night' in case Prince Charles should sit in the front row and make her laugh; and the next year a pantomime in which she took the leading role as Cinderella.

After these entertainments the Queen laid on tea for all the performers and parents, and before each Guide Meeting two of the children came in turn to tea in the Palace schoolroom—occasions when the hubbub and laughter were so uninhibited that once when there was a State Visit the Queen sent a message to say she would be very grateful for a little less noise that week, as the King in question was staying in a room close by.

The Guides went to camp in both 1962 and 1963. Five days under canvas combined fun with plenty of hard work, and there the Princess found a new freedom. Inevitably there was a detective staying nearby to keep a look-out for intruders, and obligingly ready to help out with camp chores, but otherwise she could identify completely with the other girls.

Apart from practical Guiding the Princess, young as she was, seized the opportunity to learn something of a kind of life from which she was so far removed. Very anxious to fit in, she always did her utmost to be at one with them. And in turn these lively, uncomplicated companions accepted her, liked her, respected her personality— and enlightened her with an entirely natural candour on any aspect or expression for which she demanded an explanation.

They found her excellent company, and especially appreciated the family gift for mimicry—a talent that the Queen uses almost unconsciously, and which is highly developed in both Prince Charles and Princess Margaret. This was being put to good use on the night Princess Anne was discovered delivering to the inmates of her tent a hilarious parody, of a particularly pompous sermon which they had suffered that Sunday morning. An intense dislike of pretentiousness, or of insincerity in words or behaviour, including any directed towards her position rather than herself as a person, is an intrinsic part of the Princess's make-up.

Her Guide officers found the Princess as noisy and fun-loving as the rest of the Company, but showing also a thoughtfulness towards others more adult than is usual in an eleven- to twelve-year-old. She would cheerfully volunteer for any job, even the unpleasant one of cleaning latrines, and was always the first to help, unasked, with heavy tasks such as carrying the big crates of milk and dustbins of hot water. The Company spent one afternoon ferrying, in turn and very much 'according to the book', a home-made raft across a lake. When the Captain embarked on this rather rickety craft, Princess Anne was foremost in livening up the proceedings by urging another officer to go on board as well—roaring with laughter when her hopes materialized and the raft capsized, but also the first to help fish out her dripping superiors.

The Princess has retained her sense of fun, if in a slightly less boisterous form, and she is always an asset at parties. These have ceased to rank quite as highly amongst her amusements as they did just before and after she first left school, but she enjoys dancing of any kind from Scottish to the latest teenage craze, so long as the tune is familiar. Her idea of an evening's real entertainment is a ball north of the border—a full-blooded affair, providing the 'best exercise ever', such as the annual Highland Games Ball at Oban where, in 1969, she danced till the early hours.

Princess Anne knows most of the reels danced regularly, and reckons that if necessary she can also cope with the complicated ones that are done only now and again. But whatever the style of dancing, she does it well—a legacy of

a natural rhythm, allied to the tuition started when she was only three and first joined Miss Vacani's weekly dancing class, held at the Palace for Prince Charles.

These classes were also partly the source of the good deportment and youthful dignity Princess Anne displayed as a child bridesmaid, a role she undertook at the weddings of her cousins Lady Pamela Mountbatten and the Duke of Kent and, when she was fourteen, at the Greek Royal wedding in Athens. The Princess was only ten when she was chief bridesmaid at the marriage of Princess Margaret and Mr Anthony Armstrong-Jones at Westminster Abbey. In a long, elegant gown, and with her hair dressed high in classical style, Princess Anne presented a charming portent of the years to come, adding to an occasion memorable for its beauty.

In 1956 both Prince Charles and Princess Anne had their first taste of the live theatre, in the form

personally 'involved', or to find any underlying message of 'lovely freedom'. Audience participation was part of the climax to the show, and on that night the final musical number was repeated several times—an obvious 'dare' to Princess Anne. When she accepted the challenge and went on stage with her party to dance for a few minutes with the cast, it caused a lot of publicity, but in fact the Princess had spent some time tossing up which was worse—the possibility of 'getting stick' afterwards, or of being 'called chicken' . . . this latter an insult she felt she could not take!

Much of the life of the Royal Family seems to be lived against a background of bands and martial music. Queen Victoria inaugurated the custom of the lone piper who marches up and down outside royal residences each morning at nine o'clock. And the skirl of his bagpipes and swing of his kilt are as familiar to Princess Anne, heard and seen against the settings of the ancient walls at Windsor or the grey façade of Buckingham Palace, as they are under the rain-washed Scottish skies of Balmoral. In London, during the Guard-changing ceremony, there is a tuneful if intrusive interlude by the band, rendered directly below the windows of her sitting-room; and most Palace festivities are staged to the accompaniment of a military band. It is, however, doubtful if years of this melodious backcloth have had much bearing on the Princess's addiction to her radio. She has it on whenever possible and dislikes being anywhere without it. She is very much a girl of her time, and a transistor and pop music are as essential a part of her scene as they are for ninety per cent of her generation.

The Princess 'encourages herself' to buy classical records, and would probably acquire more given the time and inclination to sit in her room and listen to them—plus a record-player a little less 'grotty' than her present one. As it is she makes no special effort to listen to this type of music, but enjoys hearing any piece she knows, without sharing Prince Charles's absorbing interest in classical music. In the meantime she collects

of a charity Dancing Matinée at the Scala which they attended with Princess Margaret, followed by a Christmas pantomime, *Dick Whittington*, with their parents. As they grew older the occasional play or film was fitted into the holidays, but remained in the category of 'treats'.

The Princess goes to the theatre or movies when there is something she especially wishes to see—or maybe now and then because her contemporaries have suggested that obviously *she* would not be allowed to go to *that!*

Her tastes are wide, but not particularly intense or intellectual. Her criterion is that the show should provide good entertainment, and this was her verdict on *Hair*, the first of the controversial musicals to reach London. Princess Anne enjoyed this show, especially the music, finding it a totally non-serious bit of fun, but nothing to 'get worked up about'. Parts of it seemed to her unnecessary to the general theme, and she failed to become

pop discs, which she can also listen to in her car as cassettes.

Music lessons began when she was six, but despite the grand piano in her sitting-room, Princess Anne declares that her playing has seldom amounted to much more than 'tickling the keyboard' now and again, a viewpoint not entirely shared by the music mistress at Benenden. In her last two years at school the Princess was responsible for the percussion in the school orchestra—again exhibiting good rhythm, combined with the ability to count 153 bars of music before coming in with her own particular 'dong'!

As for more strenuous pastimes, Prince Philip has taught all his children to swim, a session in the Palace pool often proving a popular diversion after tea. Princess Anne continued her swimming at boarding school, in the bracing if chilly waters of a bath that was only heated in her last term. She is now a strong, competent swimmer, well at home in the water if without quite the aptitude of Prince Charles.

The Princess has a love of the sea second only to riding, and it has always played a part in her life. Unfortunately she is 'an appallingly bad sailor', but one who considers being sea-sick 'awfully stupid' and, always hopeful of getting less susceptible, refuses to take any form of remedy as it would be 'admitting defeat all round'.

She was only four when she and Prince Charles made their first voyage in the Royal yacht *Britannia*, journeying out to Tobruk to meet the Queen and Prince Philip on the homeward leg of their ·Commonwealth Tour of 1954. The Princess now remembers little of the trip, except for the two delightful little models of the yacht which she and her brother pedalled about the decks, and the friendly sailors always ready to answer questions and explain how things worked.

The next year the children were again on board, this time cruising off the British coast as far up as Aberdeen—a holiday during which they had the chance to try out their father's new speedboat at Milford Haven, and which included all the

fun of numerous fishing expeditions, boating, and picnics ashore when they anchored, as usual, by day.

Britannia is a real haven of privacy for the Royal Family. Princess Anne has always loved the gay informality of life on board, with the chance to vary doing nothing whatever with hearty games of deck tennis and hockey, and all overlaid with the traditional, wonderful hospitality of the Navy.

The Princess's birthday comes during the holidays in Scotland, and is often celebrated, at least in part, at sea. On the day she was six she was cruising (her third time in *Britannia*) amongst the Western Isles. Her nineteenth birthday was spent sailing up and down the Norwegian fiords in the Royal yawl *Bloodhound*, the yacht which was sold in the autumn of 1969. These were eight days of glorious freedom when she and Prince Charles played absurd games, which included chasing each other around the deck like a couple of ten-year-olds.

There is the same elemental speed and spice of danger in handling a boat as there is in dealing with a horse, and the two sports provide members of the Royal Family with most of their too few opportunities to get right away on their own. Prince Philip took his elder children sailing on the Scottish lochs even before *Bloodhound* came on the scene about six or seven years ago. Since then, Princess Anne has enjoyed learning seamanship in company with her father, brother, and other members of the crew, consisting of the Duke's Treasurer, Rear-Admiral Sir Christopher Bonham-Carter, an ex-Petty Officer Sailing Master who looked after the yacht and an Able Seaman loaned from *Britannia*. Cruising from A to B, hooking up somewhere for the night and setting off again next day, they have explored much of the west coast of Scotland, and the lovely areas around Campbelltown and the Caledonian Canal.

No one has specifically taught the Princess how to sail, but she has picked up enough from watching her father and the crew to be able to enjoy

lending a hand in whatever there is to be done—helping to get the sails up and down, handling sheets when the wind or course changes and taking her trick at the helm. She has twice accompanied Prince Philip to Cowes Week, and has been on board *Bloodhound* when racing. But although she has sailed in *Coweslip*, her father's racing dinghy takes a crew of only two and in competitions these need to be a couple of strong men.

As a child Princess Anne was always overflowing with surplus energies. When she was six she had the opportunity to work off some of these at a weekly gym class. In 1961 she took skating lessons for two months at the Richmond Rink, and followed them up with more skating the next year.

Ski-ing, which incorporates much the same idea of speed and savour of danger as riding and sailing, appeals to Princess Anne as another 'fantastic' sport. She first tried it when she was fourteen and Prince Philip took her and Prince Charles to Liechtenstein, staying in a house that was only about an hour's drive from four different ski centres. Despite rather too much attention from the Press, this enjoyable holiday confirmed the Princess in her wish to add ski-ing to her other sporting achievements, and she spent three days of her next ski-ing holiday at Davos with a group of school friends.

Three years later, in the spring of 1969, Princess Anne flew out from Heathrow to Val d'Isère, the famous French ski-ing resort, with a party of a dozen or so young people. The Princess's natural 'nerve' and balance helped to make her an apt pupil, but she was no more immune to tumbles and laughable mishaps than any other novice. She was delighted to pass the stage of scrabbling about in the snow all the time trying to reorientate herself, and decided she was really getting on when she could fall over and get up almost in one movement—although she thought that 'sitting down promptly' was still the best method of avoiding real trouble.

HorsES OF EVERY TYPE, FROM THOSE used in ceremonial to her own 'Eventers' of today, are part of the background to Princess Anne's life. From the nursery windows she could watch the well-groomed police horses, on duty each morning helping to control the crowds that gathered for the Changing of the Guard. Or wait for the Household Cavalry black chargers that daily wheeled to jingle between the Queen Victoria Monument and the Palace en route for Whitehall—their advent announced, when the Queen was in residence, by the louder clatter of the more numerous Long Guard and lilting notes of a Royal Trumpet Salute, rendered by a Trumpeter on a grey horse.

No doubt the Queen got as much pleasure as her small daughter from showing her the riding hacks at Windsor, the foals and young stock at Sandringham, and the Highland and Fell ponies up at Balmoral. As the children got older, the Queen took them both to watch horse shows, and the Cross Country phase of the annual Three-Day Event at Badminton has long been a private and enjoyable outing for the Royal Family.

From an early age the Princess knew the famous Windsor Greys, not only from seeing them in all their splendour of State harness on ceremonial occasions, but also from visiting them in their stalls in the Royal Mews just around the corner from Buckingham Palace.

Too young to attend even that short part of the solemn, moving Coronation ceremony to which Prince Charles was taken, the Princess watched the magnificent, historic procession from the Palace windows, afterwards joining her parents on the balcony for the Fly Past. A few days later she and her brother were bowling along to

Horse Guards' Parade in an open barouche behind a pair of Windsor Greys. They were being escorted by the Queen Mother and Princess Margaret to see the Queen, splendid in her adapted uniform of Colonel-in-Chief of a Guard's Regiment, and mounted side-saddle on the police horse Winston, take the salute at the annual Trooping the Colour.

Princess Anne remembers how, as a small girl attached to a piece of string for safety, she enjoyed the long afternoons spent watching polo up at Smith's Lawn during summer weekends at Windsor. She recalls the thrill of seeing her father thundering down the field on his sweat-streaked pony, the air full of the thud-thud of galloping hooves, and the pithy expressions not supposed to be remembered by any little girl. There was all the fun of running out between chukkas with the Queen and Prince Charles to help stomp in the hoof-pitted turf, and the ultimate pride in being allowed to 'hold' a pony.

The pleasure of afternoons like these has never waned, so that now Princess Anne has a keen eye for the niceties of one of the toughest and most exciting of all games, with a knowledgeable summing-up of a player's skill and a pony's ability. Nowadays she sometimes has the added enjoyment of cheering on both Prince Philip and Prince Charles.

The Queen taught her daughter the rudiments of riding, on a Shetland pony, when the Princess was about three. Later, when at Windsor, Princess Anne had lessons with Miss Sybil Smith, whose father instructed Her Majesty as a child. William, a little roan from Ireland, and Green-sleeves, a Welsh mare, were two of the children's much-loved first ponies. Later came Bandit, the grey 'Welshman' with which both Princess Anne

and Prince Charles had much fun, competing successfully in various activities of the Garth Pony Club in Berkshire after they became members in 1962.

From the beginning the Princess showed above average 'nerve' and the same instinctive 'feel for a horse' as the Queen, and with such an equine environment it is scarcely surprising that she quickly became as 'horse mad' as any of the thousands of other little girls whose world revolves round their ponies. In this particular case her interest later provided the Princess with one of the first necessities for someone who lives so much in the public eye—a hobby and relaxation during which she can be just herself, judged on her own ability with no regard to her position, and during which she can capture occasionally the rare and valued sensation of being truly 'away out on her own'.

Even with ponies the Princess was never over-indulged. By the time she was a teenager she could, within reason, take her pick of the Windsor hacks, but as a child there was never more than one pony each for her and her brother,

and they shared Bandit between them. Both children were presented with saddles and bridles by the County Borough of Walsall and the Loriner's Company, but unlike some young people nowadays they had no selection of 'tack' for different aspects of the sport.

The Princess rode around the royal parks and grounds wearing, as she usually does now, an old pair of jeans; and waged the perennial argument common to most horse-minded families as to whether she should, or would, wear a hard riding cap. In public she was always correctly turned out, complete with cap, her jodhpurs and jacket indistinguishable from hundreds of others. On rainy days the Princess rarely wore a riding 'mack'; she was usually to be found waiting her turn to compete, or cantering through the mud, cheerfully indifferent to the discomfort of being soaked. Whatever the weather or however long the day, there has never been any question of handing pony or horse over to a groom for saddling up or putting back in the trailer—like the Queen, Princess Anne prefers doing things for herself.

She used to spend many enjoyable hours just 'messing about' round the stables at Windsor, always hopeful of trying out a youngster or new arrival, and occasionally unpopular with the stud groom for removing some animal without his knowledge during the staff dinner hour. Such an occasion was the day she joined the Queen—who was exercising the dogs close by the Castle walls—with Pride, an Arabian horse presented by King Hussein, which was 'feeling a leg'. Cautioned by her mother to take him quietly the Princess rode off—next to be observed on her feet minding her little brother Andrew, while the nurserymaid ostensibly in charge of the Prince was being carted by Pride away across the Castle golf-course, on an obvious bee-line for his stable and lunch! Despite the Princess's ingenuous explanation, 'Well . . . she asked me if she could . . .' it was an escapade not viewed with much favour by the Queen, who saw to it

that her daughter herself made good the damaging hoof-marks. A lesson soon forgotten, since only recently the Queen was forced to open a window in the Castle and implore the Princess to remove a horse from off the lawn!

Princess Anne's interest in competitive riding turned towards Eventing as far back as 1962, when High Jinks, an excellent 'all-round' brown pony from Ireland, came into her life. After encouraging ventures in a few Hunter Trials, shows and gymkhanas, the pair made a number of entries, at Pony Club level, into the tough field of Horse Trials, the form of equitation that now most appeals to the Princess.

For several years during the Easter holidays, Colonel John Miller, the Crown Equerry—who is responsible for all the royal horses and cars—organized various mounted amusements in Windsor Park for Prince Charles and his sister. In 1963 this took the form of a small One-Day Event which, to the Queen's embarrassment, was won by her daughter.

For most of the terms that Princess Anne was at Benenden, High Jinks was kept at Moat House, a well-known riding establishment near the school. The pony profited by the training he received there, and for the Princess, all school games and outdoor activities really took second place to the weekly riding lesson she was given at Moat House. Her instructor was Mrs Hatton-Hall, who started the riding school some years ago and, as Cherry Kendall, was a renowned competitive rider. She has long been a member of the Senior Judges' Panel, up to the high Prix St Georges standard in dressage.

It was at Moat House that Princess Anne was grounded in the sport she is now tackling so successfully at adult level, and it was here that her enthusiasm was initially aroused.

Like most children the Princess was at first more concerned with jumping and going hello-bellow across country than with the finer arts of schooling and dressage, and she took a mischievous delight in disrupting her class at intervals, by pinching Jinks behind the saddle so that he bucked! She usually rode her own pony, but also gained experience with a variety of the riding school horses and ponies, sometimes competing successfully with them in the five yearly Moat House competitions.

In the last two years Princess Anne rode with Mrs Hatton-Hall she really began to appreciate

that dressage, correctly applied, and clearly understood by both rider and horse, is the basis of all good equitation. The hard work she put in to achieve the high standard required for an equine quadrille enabled her to be one of the team of four from the Battle and District Riding Club who, dressed as Georgian noblemen, performed in the Eldonian Quadrille Championship at the Horse of the Year Show in October, 1968—to become reserve champions.

High Jinks continued to partner the Princess in competitions until the spring of 1968, when Mrs Alan Oliver, wife of the famous show jumper, began to help her with Eventing, and Princess Anne acquired her first horse, Purple Star. Now, in the role of pampered and beloved 'family pony', Jinks remains a constant and willing companion on the Princess's light-hearted scampers in the beautiful environs of her country homes.

By the autumn of 1969 Princess Anne was successfully competing with the three Event horses which she keeps at Mrs Oliver's stables near Bracknell, in Berkshire.

Purple Star was the first, selected about eighteen months previously by Mrs Oliver, from a choice of two offered by Colonel Miller, both the offspring of his ex-Olympic mare, Stella. This attractive 15.3-hand bay gelding was almost a novice, but he seemed the perfect type to take over from a pony, and as a first partner in the very much sterner world of adult competition. He is a three-quarter-bred, not over-large for someone as tall as Princess Anne, but a great character. He proved self-confident and quick thinking in his jumping, with a pony's cleverness at extricating himself from trouble. He bucks and plays up whenever inclined, particularly before a competition, and is always ready to 'take the micky' out of a rider forgetful of his over-developed sense of equine humour.

In those days the Princess was still at school, and only started competing with Purple Star during the Easter holidays of 1968. She began

with a couple of Pony Club competitions, which proved very encouraging, and then rode in her first adult Event, a Novice Class at the Windsor Horse Trials in which they finished seventh.

The Princess arrived at Mrs Oliver's with the good seat and balance acquired under the tuition received at Moat House. She is by nature a happy and confident rider and horses go well for her, as they do for the Queen. She was used to riding and coping with different types of animals, but had little technical knowledge and lacked the experience of training and schooling. Mrs Oliver, who has schooled and trained many Eventing horses as well as teaching their owners, was also a pupil of Mrs Gold, the Olympic

Dressage Rider. She has helped Princess Anne enormously with the essential schooling side of riding, but it is quite untrue that the Princess's horses are produced for her, and that all she has to do is to climb aboard and 'press the right button'. To succeed in Eventing horse and rider must combine, and the rider must fully appreciate the horse's physical capabilities and mental reactions. This is something that is only achieved by much mutual hard work.

Princess Anne has inherited her mother's quick understanding of what is being put over to her. She soon appreciates the feel of a horse and of what is required, and a natural rhythm in her riding, particularly across country, enables her

to ride her horses into their fences without pushing them out of balance, and in this way gives them a great feeling of security.

The Princess has the right approach to competitive riding. She goes in 'all out to win', but will not risk her horse just for the chance of being placed. She can be in a commanding position in the dressage and show jumping phases of an Event, and still go sensibly across country—fast enough to let her horse realize what it is about, but willing to lose time points, if necessary, on patches of bad going. She will always forgive the horse making mistakes, but is less charitable with herself and very honest in assessing the causes if she has not done well. She is not in the least nervous, and although like anyone else becomes 'strung up' before a competition, contrives to hide the fact. She accepts falls as

part of the game and has the 'guts' to get up quickly and continue.

It has been a help to the Princess being involved in the sort of 'stable life' where other people are going off to competitions. There she can see how a horse can go well one day with someone and fail the next—the inevitable outcome of dealing with creatures of flesh and blood—and realize that however much one dislikes being beaten, this is 'life with horses'. She has acquired a philosophical outlook and ability to get a correct assessment of the situation, and no longer worries when things go wrong. Clicking press cameras do not bother her as much as they used to—unless they distract her horse from the job in hand. She has learned to shrug off the unfairness of a report like that printed after she won the Windsor Horse Trials in 1969, when it was

suggested that she 'knows the course like the back of her hand . . . goes round it every day'. The truth was that Princess Anne had not ridden over a single one of the jumps since the previous year, when she did so with all the other competitors, and on a different horse.

A few months after the advent of Purple Star, a 16.2 thoroughbred, Royal Ocean, arrived from Ireland. Doublet, the youngest of the Princess's trio, belongs to the Queen, who bred him out of an Argentine polo-pony mare. Doublet was destined as a polo pony for Prince Philip—but to the Queen's dismay he grew to nearly 16.2 hands, which is far too big for the game.

Princess Anne at first found this sensitive, good-looking chestnut difficult to get on with. By the autumn Events of 1969, however, the two were on very good terms. They shared a lot of success, including a sixth in the final of the Midland Bank sponsored novice championship at Chatsworth, where the company was top-class, and where Princess Anne and Doublet achieved a splendid Dressage test for 25 penalty points and a clear round on the stiff cross-country course.

The Princess may occasionally manage to school her horses five or six times in the week, but of necessity there are usually big gaps in her training programme and this puts her at a great disadvantage.

Princess Anne has got the potential, and interest, to be very good indeed at competitive riding. By the end of the Eventing season of 1969 she had qualified for Badminton—which necessitates winning a minimum of £12 and completing two Events at Intermediate standard. But in these days the competition is so 'hot' that for anything approaching International level, an everyday, whole-hearted training programme is a necessity. And this is something that the Princess, with her appreciation of duty coming before inclination, knows to be an impossibility.

To every young girl comes that moment when school and school topics are suddenly insufficient and she longs for wider horizons, new pursuits, new clothes, new interests to discuss.

Princess Anne appeared to reach this stage when she was about seventeen. The school holidays had always been spent in predominantly adult company, and from the age of about fifteen onwards she was gradually included in more formal aspects of royal life. It required considerable adjustment to attend the Opening of Parliament in an official capacity or converse at a Palace banquet on a level with distinguished guests, and then return to Benenden in the role once more of obedient schoolgirl.

Princess Anne left Benenden in July 1968. Schooldays finished, the present and future offered exciting prospects, but over both hung the weighty question, where to . . . from here?

Possibly those first few months were something of an anti-climax, highlighting a problem that the Queen sees clearly: that for all the royal innovations and modernization of the past years, Her Majesty's life and environment have not, and cannot, change as much as other people's. This makes the gap between 'inside' and 'outside' wider and more difficult for her children to adapt to. Also the Princess, straight from the somewhat cloistered, organized existence of a boarding school, was suddenly faced with the unfamiliar question of how to fill her days.

Her riding of course took up some of her time. There was no lack of parties, and at that time it was easy to get out and about in London, both by day and in the evening, without exciting too much attention. Her own car, a blue Rover 2000, was a belated eighteenth-birthday present that arrived in October 1968, so that she could drive herself where she wished. She was meeting plenty of people, but she had not known the majority long enough for them to come into the category of genuine friends. Her school friends, with whom she had enjoyed five years of comparative liberty, were then first savouring a freedom impossible for one in the Princess's position. At school she herself had been able to get around to do many things that were no longer feasible, and inevitably the restrictions, unremarked before living away from home, loomed larger.

The Princess possesses an independence unthought of by the Queen when she was a girl, but of necessity it falls far short of that demanded by most girls of her generation, with their own flats and their resolve to lead their own lives.

Never one to cry for the moon, Princess Anne's commonsense philosophy is on the lines of, 'O.K. . . . so I've got these limitations to my life—let's see what I can do with what I've got, within them'. But at that time, with the idea of university fading, there seemed no suitable work for which she could train, which would utilize her innate enthusiasm and energies. It had not yet been decided when she would commence her public life.

Even in the unlikely event of Princess Anne spending some of her time on the domestic arts, housekeeping or housework in homes the size of the royal residences, as the Queen points out, is scarcely practicable! As a child the Princess liked to try her hand at ironing—when she could get near the ironing board—but washing clothes is not her idea of fun. Knitting has always been anathema and sewing not much better. Prince

Philip cooks whenever he can, but his daughter has not inherited this taste to any degree. She passed her cooking test as a Guide, and of the cooking she did at school, says that she 'loved it and messed about a great deal' but 'did need a lot of "Is this all right now?" sort of aid'. Certain nowadays that she would be unable to remember the first thing about those lessons, the Princess reckons scrambled eggs and the barbecuing she does on picnics in Scotland under her father's instruction about represent the limits of her culinary abilities.

Left to herself, Princess Anne would probably have followed her inclination to wear clothes until they were 'past usefulness'. Even now the Queen says her daughter has sometimes to be encouraged to go shopping for new ones. Much of her good taste was formed in the years when her clothes were chosen principally by the Queen, but after the age of about fourteen the Princess, helped by Miss Anderson, took time off in the school holidays to shop for her own ready-mades. The selection would be sent to the Palace 'on approval' but even in those days, although the Queen expressed preferences, she would never actually veto anything Princess Anne particularly liked.

Much the same course was adopted when Princess Anne first began experimenting with some of the trendy clothes of her age-group. The Queen appreciates that, largely, the young have to learn for themselves, and if some of the Princess's earlier essays in suitable attire were less successful than others, she was left to discover the fact for herself.

With her sense of humour she has always been fully capable of appreciating that, if she appeared neat, tidy and formally dressed to watch polo, the public would demand to know 'why Princess Anne is not allowed to dress like her own generation'. And if she did just that, there was an outcry about Princess Anne going around in *such* clothes.

Apart from a few pleas, and her far more frequent unqualified approval, the Queen has not attempted to influence the Princess's choice of clothes since her daughter first began shopping around for an all-adult wardrobe.

In fact, in all matters concerning their children the Queen and Prince Philip have an unhampering, sensible approach, not setting out to make them into different people from what they are, but trying to help them to make the most of whatever it is they actually want to do in life. Prince Philip realizes clearly that parents' assessment of their children is not necessarily either very accurate or very objective, with the added difficulty that a great many children never make up their minds what they want to do.

The Duke and his daughter are much alike in many ways, and as a child Princess Anne's sense of fun and readiness to embark on any outdoor activity put them on a very companionable footing. But a father and daughter relationship is seldom static. They go through periods when they are very much on the same wave-length, and phases when they certainly do not see eye to eye; and Prince Philip has also had to adjust to that bewildering moment when one's daughter is a child one day and then, seemingly overnight, blossoms into a grown-up, attractive young woman of independent views.

As the Princess has grown up, advice from both parents has always been available, but the final decision has been left to her. She considers this attitude a very good one because they give advice without categorically saying 'yes' or 'no', which ensures that she thinks out the problem for herself. This normally precludes her doing something foolish, because it would then be entirely her own fault. 'If you make a fool of yourself, you can't then lay it on your parents!'

By the early spring of 1969 Princess Anne was fully appreciating the added independence that her own car afforded her. New acquaintances had by then become real friends, and the pleasing fact that she could make friends easily added to her self-confidence and enjoyment of other people's company. She had deliberately set out to overcome her genuine difficulty in producing polite small-talk, and gone for ever were the occasional agonizing meals at Balmoral when the young Princess Anne used to sit in stony silence, unable to find a word for some unknown elderly guest seated beside her. She is quick to absorb much that she hears from the distinguished people who come to the Palace, and to form her own opinions, and the Princess's conversation soon developed into the kind of stimulating discussion that today makes eminent people of all age-groups delight in her company.

She had lost weight, an achievement owing nothing to the variety of stringent diets wished on her by the Press but solely through eating less and taking a lot of fairly violent exercise with a horse! The rewarding result was the very attractive, slim figure of today, on which clothes before deemed perfectly adequate began to look wrong or no longer fitted. So Princess Anne went shopping—looking, trying-on, and buying off-the-peg in chain stores and Regent Street, Bond Street and the King's Road, Knightsbridge or anywhere she fancied, striding out in head-scarf, mini-skirt and long boots, often un-recognized—setting an unheard-of precedent for any daughter of a British monarch.

If she knows what she is after, Princess Anne sometimes goes to the shops with only a detective in attendance, but otherwise appreciates the help-ful comments of a friend, often the Lady-in-Waiting loaned her by the Queen until the Princess one day perhaps acquires her own 'team'. She can find it as difficult to make up her mind as any other woman, but has very definite ideas on what suits her, shooting down the hypocritical sales talk of the 'but that looks *so* nice on you . . .' line with her usual down-to-earth honesty.

The length of the Princess's hemline varies according to the garment. There is no chopping off a couple of inches to spoil the line of a beautiful dress just for the sake of being 'with it', but luck and good judgement seem always to produce a length that shows her nice legs to advantage, and that is youthfully trendy without offending the older generation.

Many of today's fashions are ugly as well as eccentric, and it is not always easy to find an outfit suitable for a public engagement that is also young and up-to-the-minute modern. But even before Princess Anne had embarked on a public life of her own she was establishing that flair for the uncluttered, gay clothes in clear, glowing colours that quickly attracted and held the world's admiration.

With public functions came the hats. The Princess has always loathed wearing a hat, and for her first appointment, at Pirbright with the Welsh Guards, wore the small black cap, chain-decorated across the peak, that constituted almost her entire collection of possible headgear. Before her next engagement, in Warwickshire, Princess Anne had been persuaded to visit a hat-shop in Belgravia. It was not over-difficult for the imaginative hatter to convince his new client that if she had to wear a hat at all it might as well be an 'important' one, but it was touch and go whether the Princess would actually appear in her first buy, a fetching black sombrero. The fact that the public liked it and that she herself felt good in it, boosted the wearer's morale, and from that day her hats have been news.

The range is wide. There have been small hats like the striped jockey cap with its cheeky pom-pom that put traditional 'picture' hats to rout at a wet Ascot; a head-hugger fashioned from giant daisies; simple berets perched to one side or at the back of the head; and the stunning pill-box with its chic fan-like decorations worn to the Prince of Wales's Investiture. But the majority of the Princess's hats are large ones, with big eye-catching brims dashingly slanted or turned up at the back, and trimmed with brilliant-coloured scarves or bows, or with the neat buckles that adorn many of her clothes. Mostly they are quite unlike the off-the-face headgear traditional for royal ladies—and to begin with not altogether popular with press photographers, who were unwilling to offset their becoming line against the occasional shadow on the wearer's face.

Imitation may be the sincerest form of flattery, but the Princess feels an understandable female irritation at seeing thousands of copies, at around 35s. each, of some hat she wore only shortly before, and which cost her a price 'not to be sniffed at'. Nor will she bow to the outmoded but still occasionally resurrected notion that Royalty should not be seen in the same outfit twice. Hats are treated like all her clothes—if she likes them she wears them. Having set a trend that has caught on with her age-group, Princess Anne has become the hatters' 'pin-up' girl. But maybe, as the Queen jokingly suggests, the future size of her daughter's headgear will be determined by the number of hatboxes that can be carried around once the Princess starts to travel!

A hairdresser comes to the Palace to create a coiffeur for Princess Anne on big occasions, but more often she does her hair herself. And since it is as strong-minded as its owner, the Princess finds that her hair seldom goes the same way twice—one week 'just flapping about', having to be tied back the next, and sometimes being 'half up and half down'.

At the beginning of her public life the Princess went to a beautician to learn how to apply her make-up properly. She likes to experiment with make-up in the evening, and try for different effects, but wears as little as possible, and often none at all, during the day.

For all the royal ladies, a hair-do and make-up that require the minimum of attention are a necessity, both for the long hours when they are on public duty and for the variety of transport by which they arrive—which can be most things from a carriage and horses to a helicopter.

Because time is one of the Royal Family's most precious commodities, they use flying as an increasingly popular method of transport. Princess Anne had her first taste of it in May 1955, when she and Prince Charles were taken up in a helicopter for a buzz over Windsor. A month later they returned from Scotland in a Viking of the Queen's Flight, flying from Dyce, outside Aberdeen, to London Airport.

Now that the Princess has embarked on public engagements of her own, a plane is sometimes the only solution to long distances that have to be covered quickly, but unfortunately increasing familiarity has made no difference to the fact that, according to herself, Princess Anne is 'the world's worst flyer'! She blames her ears for just not being attuned to the motion, whether in the air or on the sea. She admits she is capable of feeling ill in a car unless driving herself, and concludes that the only transport with which she feels completely happy is a horse. 'I don't actually feel sick on that...'

The precise starting date for the Princess's public life came almost by chance. Her first public engagement was on 1 March 1969 when Prince Philip was unable to present the customary leeks to the Welsh Guards on St David's Day, and Princess Anne was asked in his stead.

The Princess had already been accompanying her parents to various State and civic functions, but it is of course a different matter when the entire ceremony centres on oneself. At the time of that first date with the Welsh Guards she was only eighteen, and she considers she was lucky to get such a gentle introduction to this public part of her life—finding the disarming friendliness and shared laughter of the Mess supplemented by the enthusiastic reception she got from the troops. This is something that, as the Princess says, one *could* perhaps get blasé about in time, but which she is sure she never will. The moment for them all to cheer may perhaps be written down on a bit of paper, but she finds the genuine warmth

delightful, and it 'makes you feel a hundred times better'!

With her interest in all that goes on, and the marvellous chance to see and learn something new each time, Princess Anne thoroughly enjoys the very different assignments that now come her way. On 25 April she spent a full day in Warwickshire. A visit to the Equestrian Centre at Stoneleigh Abbey brought her into a most congenial and familiar atmosphere. Opening the nearby Young Farmers' Club Centre at Kenilworth the same afternoon gave contact with an age-group with which she quickly identifies—and the gift of a charming, old-fashioned 'corn-dolly'. But it was perhaps the morning's tour of the Rover Car Works at Solihull that especially caught her imagination.

Princess Anne is basically mechanically minded, with a 'general fascination for things that go... chug', and she combines the unusual concerns of schooling horses with the pipe-dream of taking a course in engineering. Her first effort at driving a machine was at the age of four, when she steered a plane-towing tractor along the flight deck of H.M.S. *Eagle* at anchor in Grand Harbour, Malta. She learned to drive a car at a very early age, taught by Prince Philip within the safe and legitimate confines of Windsor Park. Like all the Royal Family, Princess Anne drives well and passed the Driving Test with ease at the first attempt. Not long after this she coped competently with the real and unpleasant emergency of a shattered windscreen when driving herself on the fast lane of the M4. Her driving experience now embraces many different vehicles, from the Go-Karts she races with her brothers around the lawns and paths at Windsor and Balmoral, to the 79-seater, 9-ton double-decker bus she drove after opening the Road Transport Industry Training Board's education and training centre at High Ercall, Shropshire, on 10 September. Not to mention the 50-ton tank she drove when she visited her Regiment in Germany! She has travelled in an even greater variety, including the British Rail Seaspeed hovercraft on which she unveiled her own name, *The Princess Anne*, on 21 October, before taking a trip from the Dover Hoverport out to the Goodwin Sands and back.

Walking round one of the Rover factory assembly sheds at Solihull that morning, her ears assailed by the hissing, banging and clacking essential to industrial mass production, the Princess missed nothing of the endless conveyor belts, sliding by with cars in all stages of embryonic growth. She inspected the battered aspect of one of the prototypes that are deliberately hurled against concrete walls to gauge what they 'can take', and sighed enviously at the rakish good looks of a super sports car. Flashes from press cameras at close range inside the cab of a huge, experimental gas-turbine lorry did nothing to disturb the Princess's happy absorption in starting the engine, and finding out the functions of the numerous controls.

At Shepton Mallet, driven, standing in an open Land Rover, amongst the clapping crowds, the striped tents and gay flags of the Bath and West Agricultural Show on 29 May, the Princess was taken to see many things to catch her interest— New Zealand sheep-shearers, stripping reluctant ewes of their heavy, greasy fleeces in record time; parades of sheep and cattle, where she learned the right shape for a prize-winner, and saw more different breeds than she knew existed. There were the entrancing offspring of every domestic animal from a Shetland foal to a Muscovy duckling shown in the 'Animal Nursery'. The Royal Canadian Mounted Police were there with traditional stetsons, red jackets and shining black horses, wheeling and weaving at trot and canter with pennants fluttering from their lance-heads as they performed the split-second timing and intricate movements of their Ceremonial Ride, a spectacle now almost as well known as the famous Mounties themselves. There was even a strange collection of land-drains to inspect.

And as the day closed the Princess sat a little

but when they were . . .

wearily, eyes strained towards the sky from which came detachments of the Red Devils, the Army Parachute Jumping Team—falling and floating from the sky before spinning down like dervishes below their red, white and blue parachutes in a breathtaking display of controlled, free-fall jumping.

Princess Anne attended the first football match of her life when she presented the trophies on 26 April at the F.A. Cup Final at Wembley, where she found herself caught up in the wild excitement of the game, was mildly astonished at the players' tendency to 'act up' minor injuries, and experienced the almost frightening impact of 100,000 soccer fans entirely engrossed in roaring encouragement to their own side. The Princess made another presentation connected with sport nearly three months later when she watched the Ladies' Singles Championships on the Centre Court at Wimbledon, and was able to hand the winner's gold trophy to Ann Jones, the triumphant British player.

She attended a mass meeting of the Scotland Women's Guild in Edinburgh in May, opened a

new hospital at the Animal Health Trust's centre for small animals in Suffolk in July, and had previously delighted a startled luncheon audience at the Reception and Opening of the Festival of London Stores on 26 May with an offbeat and unroyally revealing speech about her personal shopping. 'I was tempted into Fenwicks by way of being stuck in Bond Street traffic jams . . . Selfridges supplied me with what an outraged woman described as a "zebra" coat (I've never seen a blue-and-white zebra—she must have confused me with a zebra crossing!) . . . I have bought articles in Peter Robinson's, but I do not think they are the sort of things you discuss here!'

All through 1969 the public engagements increased, while the Princess shed much of the initial slight nervousness of the time when she was 'not quite sure of the pattern, or what one ought to say'. She has learned to control a naturally quick temper and the occasional unintentionally hurtful repartee is immediately regretted. Without doubt, Princess Anne has a talent for 'saying the right thing in public'— because she talks from the heart. There is nothing in the least artificial about her, and it is one of her great qualities that she is exactly the same in manner to everyone, young, old, influential or not, and is quite incapable of ever 'talking down'. Even so it is not easy, and those who sometimes complain that the royal 'chit-chat' at public functions is uninspired should just try it for themselves. An interesting conversation with one person means missing out the next, and one can either treat them all basically the same or attempt the humanly impossible—to think up something different to say to each one, in a tight time-schedule which precludes any very searching questions.

During this 'first time round' of her public duties, Princess Anne has done much more than find an interest in things. She has become more and more involved with people, and that includes the intangible impact of a welcoming crowd. She is not by nature emotional, but no one could fail to be moved by the kind of greeting the Princess received in Newcastle on 2 May, when at her mother's suggestion she visited the Swan Hunter's yard on Tyneside to launch the s.s. *Esso Northumbria* as the Queen was unable to do so.

Despite wind and rain the crowds were out from the moment the royal plane touched down on the puddled runway at Newcastle Airport until Princess Anne boarded the London train that night. From shops and factories, housing estates and schools they came to line the wet streets—flocks of women, a sprinkling of men and hordes of excited children, with their flags and umbrellas and ingenuous warmth of welcome. They were thousands strong around the Royal Station Hotel where the Princess had lunch, and four or five deep on the pavements all the way down to Wallsend shipyard, where the yard workers and men who had actually built the ship were packed solidly between the murky river with its fringe of cranes and the massive bulk of the tanker. They were perched precariously on every available gantry, leaning on their sledge-hammers under the bulge of the hull, and dwarfed to pygmies

on the deck 65 feet above. When the Princess—standing high up on an awned dais yet still well below the bows—pressed the lock release so that the beribboned bottle of champagne smashed true against the ship's side, her voice rang out clear: 'I name this ship the *Esso Northumbria*—and may God bless all who sail in her!' There was a moment's silence when the tanker did not move, and from far down by the keel a word of advice came floating up: 'Give her a shove, Miss!' Then slowly, slowly, the great mass started to travel, gathering speed as clouds of red dust rose from the gantries, while ships' sirens wailed, helicopters roared overhead and a great shout went up, resolving into cheer upon cheer as the stern hit the water in a sheet of spray and a colossal wave swept across the river to the opposite shore.

As Princess Anne said later in the day, standing in the big blue-and-white striped marquee where she had joined 600 Swan Hunter and Esso Petroleum guests for tea, '. . . I have had the honour of launching the largest ship ever built in this country, and, for a starter, that's not bad . . .'

And for a starter on the round of royal duties it was not bad either to complete an engagement that began at noon and progressed eventually to a dinner-dance, ending with a drive to the station at 10.30 p.m. through streets where people still hunched in the rain to cheer her—without anyone during that memorable day having the least idea that Princess Anne already had the influenza that was to confine her to bed and delay her departure on the State Visit to Austria.

As PRINCESS ANNE'S PUBLIC COMMITMENTS inevitably snowball, keeping this part of her life in proportion is not always easy. Each member of the Royal Family agrees to officiate at a great number of these functions every year, but there are also an enormous number to which they have reluctantly to say 'no' and much detailed care and planning goes into those they undertake.

The duties of a Lady-in-Waiting combine that of friend, mentor and companion with a great deal of secretarial and other responsibilities. Usually the requests affecting Princess Anne arrive first on the desk of the Lady-in-Waiting on duty, who sorts them and then shows them to the Princess. Princess Anne then discusses with the Queen any invitations that she thinks might be accepted. Her Majesty may go so far as to say that, if the Princess agrees, some particular plan sounds good, but will never make a definite decision for her daughter. The Lady-in-Waiting then finds out all she can about the organization in question, if necessary seeking advice from the Home Office or the Lord-Lieutenant of the county concerned, and passes on all the information, plus any special recommendations, to the Princess.

Once an engagement is decided upon, the first preparations devolve on the Lady-in-Waiting. She informs the Lord-Lieutenant, finds out about travelling arrangements and distances between A and B, and if the commitment is abroad, has to ascertain the type of climate and clothes necessary, sometimes for six or more months ahead. She may perhaps fly out well in advance, as in the case of the Princess's assignment with the Royal Hussars in Germany, to advise on the arrangements at that end.

All public royal events are widely reported, and since royal visits greatly contribute towards maintaining contact between the monarchy and the public, their success depends a great deal on an efficient press operation. Much of the responsibility for press arrangements on royal visits, in Britain but outside London, is assumed by Regional Offices of the Central Office of Information. They make it possible for accredited reporters and photographers to be included in the small privileged Rota Party, to follow along with the Princess's entourage. This also means providing three or four official cars for their use, which move off with the royal car and police escort and leave behind any unfortunates unable to get aboard in the concerted stampede. Satisfactory arrangements for seeing and hearing have also to be made at strategic points for the much larger number of non-Rota cameramen and reporters who are obliged to remain static.

As for the royal personage concerned, these visits often include two or three different engagements in one day, usually long drives at a crawling pace through large crowds gathered for the occasion, and only relatively short intervals for relaxing away from the public gaze. And since it is a herculean feat to smile happily throughout, it is fortunate that all the Royal Family possess an exceptionally well developed sense of humour to carry them through the longest and most tiring day.

On these occasions Princess Anne can always find something to amuse or catch her fancy but, with her usual kindness of heart, hopes that it will be some predicament concerning herself, or some incident rather than a person, that strikes her as funny. She loves to laugh with people:

quite a different matter from laughing at them.

The seldom realized fact that practically all comments along the route can be clearly heard inside the royal car often provides light relief—and what girl would not be delighted to catch remarks like: 'Coo . . . what a smashing hat!'

The children who flock after Princess Anne also often supply unexpected disruptions to the most punctilious programme.

Both Prince Charles and his sister found a humorous relief from the magnificence and strain of the Prince of Wales's Investiture when, after taking leave of the Queen and the rest of the Royal Family, they were driven off in Her Majesty's special Rolls. This was the gleaming car used on occasions of state, in which nobody had ever driven before without the Queen—and in which the young Prince and Princess, seated regally on their own in the back with the roof down, felt, and looked, as the Queen told them later, just like a honeymoon couple.

Hours of formal 'good behaviour' condition anyone to an appreciation of the ridiculous, but few royal incidents rival that of the lift during the Queen's State Visit to Austria.

Her Majesty, Prince Philip and Princess Anne visited an hotel in Innsbruck for a pre-lunch reception, after an interesting but distinctly 'constitutional' morning. The lift stopped at the royal party's destination, the third floor. The liftman got out, the hotel manager got out, as did the Duke, but Princess Anne and a Lady-in-Waiting were behind the Queen as she paused to say something. At that moment the doors closed and the lift started to descend. There appeared to be no 'stop' button, and no notice that looked even remotely like the German equivalent of 'open door'. By the time the three unwilling occupants arrived back at the ground floor, their ludicrous situation had reduced Princess Anne to gales of uncontrollable laughter, and the Queen and Lady-in-Waiting, recalling Her Majesty's lifelong conviction that lifts get stuck, were almost equally hilarious. They stopped,

and when the doors parted sufficiently to reveal to the startled party waiting to ascend the laughing faces of the British Queen and her daughter, they found it equally amusing—but only the reception clerk acted. Gallantly he dashed for the doors as they began once more to close, but it was too late—and the royal party were more than relieved to see his fingers withdrawn in the nick of time.

The Queen suggested that when and wherever the lift stopped they would simply have to rush the doors, unless they wished to be there for life going up and down like yo-yos!

Back at the third floor Prince Philip was awaiting his family and appreciating the comedy, unlike the hotel manager and liftman who were by then almost out of their minds with horror. Once again the lift glided to a halt, and as the doors opened the three passengers 'took it like a steeplechase and shot out', preceded, as the Princess recounts with dramatic hyperbole, 'by a shower of "laughter" tears'!

Long before Princess Anne began her public engagements she had accepted that reasonable press coverage of the greater part of the Royal Family's life, including nowadays a considerable interest in their private life, is an essential and acknowledged 'part of the job'.

Early in 1969 the Princess met and charmed a number of young journalists at two press cocktail parties given at the Palace. The amount of interest in her doings still amazes her, and she is often entertained and amused to read different versions of her various activities in newspapers and magazines. The occasional and inevitable inaccuracies worry her little, unless they are specifically untrue or concern friends who are totally unused to this facet of publicity—and who, in the case of men friends, are also embarrassed at being publicly and lengthily discussed as possible suitors, even if they have perhaps squired the Princess on only one occasion.

The Princess is also as yet too young and uncynical not to mind hurtful stories like that printed

At Buckingham Palace after the Trooping the ▷
Colour ceremony, June 1969,
as Concorde flies over

and potatoes—gourmet's fare that was represented by an unlimited supply of dolly-mixtures and jelly-babies.

Firm in their expressed conviction that all Princesses like plenty to eat, the children pressed more and more 'food' on their compliant guest, until the poor Princess's mouth became literally gummed up with the cloying sweets and she was reduced to murmuring plaintively 'What do I do about this . . .?' A probing finger was the obvious and only possible solution, but there happened to be two press photographers crouched in one corner of the room very busily at work. When her predicament was put to them, the young men exclaimed, 'The Princess can do anything she likes . . . she's given us so many marvellous pictures!' and gallantly laid their cameras down on the floor.

in one country after she attended the 'hippy show *Hair*, when it made good news to misconstrue the incident and suggest, without a shadow of truth, that the Queen had forbidden her daughter to go, but that the Duke had bought her a ticket. This is the kind of stupid concoction that the Princess will in time learn to laugh off as the rest of her family have done.

She was also justifiably annoyed when a journalist sent in an article to be 'vetted' and then printed it in full, including the items which had been crossed out—not because the Princess objected to the context, but because they happened to be untrue.

The press photographers are openly delighted with the attractive girl who was so quick to appreciate what they wanted, and has done her best to co-operate ever since. And they respond to her ready friendliness in every way they can.

During the memorable visit to the Church of Scotland Children's Home in May, the Princess and her Lady-in-Waiting were invited to a dolls' tea-party, from which all officials were excluded. Seated on wooden boxes for chairs, the two girls partook of a feast of imaginary black pudding

Princess Anne's public appearances are certainly not limited to those she does on her own, and which, apart from other considerations, are often a great help in spreading the heavy load of royal functions—she also accompanies the Queen and Prince Philip on various occasions.

On 31 October 1967, and again the next year, the Princess drove with the Queen to the State Opening of Parliament, drawn through the London streets in the Irish State Coach, to play her part in one of those historical rites of pageantry that colour the British year. She joins the Royal Family for gala performances on stage and screen; accompanies the Queen to events like the swimming gala, organized to celebrate the centenary of the Amateur Swimming Association, held at the Crystal Palace on 15 May 1969, and in November that same year stood with her parents amongst the poppy petals fluttering down from the roof of the Albert Hall, during the British Legion Festival of Remembrance.

Ever since she was a baby, the Princess has been out on the Palace balcony with the Royal Family for the R.A.F. Fly Past, the exciting aerial spectacle that concludes the Trooping the Colour ceremony

held on the Queen's official birthday each June. In 1969 there was the added thrill of seeing and hearing Britain's Concorde, forging majestically overhead at fifteen hundred feet in the wake of the escorting R.A.F. Lightning fighters.

That year also Princess Anne had the opportunity, twice over, to absorb the unforgettable, never-failing splendour of ships of the line in review order. She was on board *Britannia* when the Queen reviewed the NATO Fleet at Spithead, as part of NATO's twentieth-anniversary celebrations on 16 May. When Her Majesty visited her Western Fleet at Torbay on 28 July the Princess heard the reverberating thunder of a 21-gun royal salute firing across the bay.

The splendours of that day were undimmed by the torrential Devon rain, which did not deter the royal party from splitting up to visit different ships. While enjoying herself on board H.M. Anti-Submarine Frigate *Eastbourne* the Princess made a first acquaintance with the traditional naval tot of grog—and found it little more to her

liking than any other spirit. That evening, when the Fleet, dressed overall with lights, acquired a different, ethereal beauty, Princess Anne was with the Queen and other members of the party on H.M.S. *Eagle* being entertained by the ship's concert party.

Since childhood the Princess has had the opportunity of meeting many of the eminent men and women who are entertained by the Queen. These have included a number of the world's Heads of State, and in the summer of 1969 Prince Charles and his sister were with the Queen and Prince Philip to greet Mr Nixon, the new President of the United States. The Prince and Princess also attend some of the functions given by Ambassadors or Foreign Embassies. Princess Anne went to the dinner-dance arranged for Miss Tricia Nixon by the American Ambassador at Claridge's Hotel on 4 July, and a fortnight later attended the luncheon given by President and Madame Kekkonen at the Finnish Embassy.

So much happened to make 1969 a memorable year for Princess Anne, but 1 July, the date of the Prince of Wales's Investiture, stood out as a day on its own for her as for all the Royal Family.

Sitting in the royal train, parked in a secret siding some miles outside Caernarvon, the Princess watched with her family on colour television the build-up to the ceremony: the gathering crowds, many of whom had spent the night camping out in the streets; the sun breaking through to highlight especially vivid contingents in the long, colourful processions—Heralds and Pursuivants of Arms in embroidered gold and scarlet tunics, sombre Welsh Sheriffs in their black eighteenth-century costumes, the peers in ermine and scarlet.

After the royal train arrived the Queen, heralded by booming guns, by the clatter of the Royal Escort of Household Cavalry and by the swelling cheers, drove to the Water Gate of Caernarvon Castle to receive the massive, symbolic key from Lord Snowdon, the Constable of the Castle. Soon after, the Queen Mother, Princess Anne and Princess Margaret went in procession to a dais within the Castle walls, and from there watched the moving ceremony of mediaeval chivalry, made even more impressive and brought into the present day by Prince Charles's sincere and active interpretation of his motto, 'Ich Dien . . . I Serve'.

Set against the grey walls and arrow slits of the ancient Castle, the scene was dominated by an oval of grey slate which held the simple thrones for the Queen, Prince Philip and the Prince of Wales, a setting enhanced a hundred times by the accompaniment of glorious-voiced Welsh choirs, and the shrill interruptions of the fanfares.

After the breaking of the Prince of Wales's personal banner and when the trumpets of the Household Cavalry sounding from the ramparts had announced his arrival at the Water Gate, Princess Anne watched her brother, unfamiliar in his uniform of the new Royal Regiment of Wales, being escorted to the scene in answer to the Queen's summons. She saw the poignant moment when he knelt in front of their mother to receive the coronet, the mantle and insignia, and when, his hands held between the Queen's, he declared himself 'her liege man of life and limb and earthly worship'. She heard him make his speech in Welsh and English, and out of all that long, stirring ceremony was most moved by the thunderous cheers when the Queen, from the gateways of the Castle, presented their Prince to the people of Wales.

As well as ceremonies and functions, Princess Anne likes accompanying her parents to some of the big sporting events. She went to the 1969 Derby and to Royal Ascot Week in June, although she is too much of a 'participant' type to share fully in the Queen's knowledgeable pleasure in racing. Like the Queen, the Princess does not bet, contending that any horse on which she might be tempted to put her money 'would drop dead at the mere thought'.

The social side to Ascot always provides an opportunity to meet plenty of friends, especially during the sojourns in the paddock, and in 1969 there was the usual enjoyable house-party at Windsor Castle. The weather that year supplied occasions for the Princess to prove that attractive ensembles can also be practical in pouring rain, and the week was highlighted for her by the traditional 'royal race'. This is a lighthearted early-morning scamper up the race-course that was inaugurated by the Queen when she was a girl and in which Her Majesty, her family, her guests and almost every horse in the Windsor Mews take part. It had, however, to be suspended for a while owing to a build-up of publicity.

In 1969 Princess Anne, riding her Eventer, Royal Ocean, took on the young Olympic rider Richard Meade, mounted on a borrowed police horse of somewhat uncertain temperament. By giving the rest of the riding party a start sufficient to clear the course, the two of them were able to stoke up a gallop beating all previous speed records for that particular contest.

May of that same year brought the Princess an

insight into the ultimate of royal protocol, when she joined the Queen and Prince Philip in Austria for her first State Visit.

Delayed for two days by a bout of influenza, the Princess flew to Vienna on the morning of Wednesday, 7 May. She arrived to a thunderstorm breaking about her from the heavens, and to a storm of friendly greetings from the appreciative Austrians, ready to take this delightful young girl straight to their hearts.

Her late arrival resulted in her missing the magnificent reception at the Schönbrunn Palace, and a brilliant evening at the State Opera, but once in Vienna the Princess plunged straight into the official programme—driving with her parents to a civic reception at the Rathaus, or Town Hall, followed by lunch with the Lord Mayor. She helped the Queen greet the 2,000 members of the Commonwealth who live in Vienna and other parts of Austria, showing a natural friendly grace that must have made her mother feel very proud. And at the evening reception at the British Embassy the Queen and her daughter, both superbly gowned, matched in looks and charm any of the many lovely women who have come to Vienna through the centuries.

The royal visitors saw something of the architectural beauties of Salzburg, and in Innsbruck, which the Queen was the first British monarch to visit since Queen Victoria, they were treated to a parade by the ceremonial Schützen companies, weatherbeaten riflemen from mountain farms, and smiling girls in the beautifully embroidered skirts of the Tyrolean peasant, their hats adorned with mountain flowers. The royal party dined in the Archbishop's Palace and drove out from the city to meet the warm-hearted people of the countryside. At Seekirchen they were very impressed by a *Kinderdorf* or Orphans' Village—where yet again Princess Anne got caught up with welcoming children.

After an appreciated visit to the State Stud at Piber, where the famous Lipizzaner horses are bred, the party returned to a reception just outside

Graz, to a castle where electricity is still unknown, and complexions glowed in the soft light of hundreds of candles. Here they were given a feast that began with tea and cakes, strawberries and cream, before proceeding to the stern realities of the main meal, washed down with an unlimited supply of red and white wine, beer and slivovitz.

Many people who go to Vienna visit the lovely sixteenth-century Baroque building called the Spanish Riding School from the Iberian blood of the first horses that were used there—the forerunners of the magnificent white Lipizzaner stallions that are famous throughout the world today.

The Spanish Riding School is the home of the pure, classical form of horsemanship that was rediscovered during the fifteenth and early sixteenth centuries, and Princess Anne was very sorry to miss the spectacular display that was put on to enchant the Queen and Prince Philip. She was, however, able to watch a practice ride and, best of all, to have the unique experience of herself riding one of the top stallions, the thirteen-year-old Siglavy Bona.

These Lipizzaner stallions, specially selected from the Piber strains for exceptional aptitude, beauty and strength, take at least five years to train in some of the movements of Haute École—which is claimed to be the uncorrupted interpretation of the highest art of riding. Every man who schools them himself undergoes ten or more years of arduous instruction before becoming a qualified *Bereiter*, and it would be impossible for any rider, however good, really to perform with a horse schooled to these exceptional standards without years of practice in the art. The quality of Princess Anne's riding, the understanding she now has of dressage and the aids, and the high standard of teaching she has received through the years, are borne out by the manner in which Siglavy Bona co-operated with the first lady rider he had ever carried.

Instructed by Colonel Johann Handler, Head of the Spanish School, the Princess was able to convey directions to an animal that, with an inadequate rider, might have refused to move at all, or have become completely confused. As it was she achieved 'flying changes'—which took a little while to get the correct timing—and amongst other movements the passage and the difficult 'piaffe'. This last is a lofty trot performed on one spot without gaining ground, which tends to throw one out of the saddle if the horse is doing it correctly and which the Princess found 'very remarkable and satisfying, if you can get it right'!

Riding is important to Princess Anne. The Queen, who acknowledges that she herself has never outgrown her real love for any equine from a Fell or Shetland pony to a racehorse, and fully appreciates her daughter's real interest and good progress in riding, yet hopes the Princess may in time find another absorbing occupation as well, a hope that is shared by Prince Philip. He too admits the achievement of becoming a top-flight rider, yet is not sure, even if Princess Anne aimed as high as competing at international level, whether it would last her through life as the substantial attainment he wishes for her.

The Princess would like to become a really successful rider, because 'It's the one thing that the world can see I can do well that's got *nothing* whatever to do with my position, or money, or anything else. If I'm good at it, I'm good at it—and not because I'm Princess Anne.'

'WHAT A DOLLY!' EXCLAIMED A disembodied, unmistakably American voice, expressing the general opinion as Princess Anne disappeared up a flight of steps to the small heli-pad where a Wessex 4 Helicopter of the Queen's Flight awaited her.

This was the occasion on 28 October 1969 of the Princess's visit to the AMOCO 'B' gas production platform—one of the rigs hired and operated by the AMOCO Group, an offshoot of International American Oil, which is a subsidiary of Standard Oil of Indiana and the eighth largest oil company in the world.

The Princess had flown in that morning, her scarlet helicopter 'chopping' across the Norfolk countryside over the shoreline and on forty miles out into the misty reaches of the North Sea—to where three Gas Council/AMOCO rigs, their stilted legs planted deep in the sea bed, are divided into separate, lonely units by many sea-miles of open water.

In coming there on that uncharacteristically calm and temperate day Princess Anne defied the superstition that women bring ill-luck to a rig. She found enough of engineering interest to occupy her enquiring mind for some time and openly revelled in the delightfully friendly and informal atmosphere of such a restricted world.

The crew of these rigs—normally about forty men on 'B' Rig—work a stint of two weeks on, followed by one week ashore. The two shifts are of twelve hours each, and although the inevitably small living space is comfortable, and the food served at the four meals per day generous even by American standards, there is little scope in the limited free time for anything other than television or card-playing. It meant a great deal

to an isolated group of men engaged on work that is hard, dirty, and always potentially dangerous, that this gay young girl in her splendid vermilion trouser-suit and jaunty hat should fly out to see their tough way of life for herself, and become so obviously absorbed in what she found.

Enveloped in a white boiler-suit, specially provided as protection against the yellowish film of oil that covers the outside surface of the rig, Princess Anne exchanged her trendy hat for the silvery safety-helmet that is obligatory wear for everyone out on top. Her initiation began with diagrams, and an explanation of a procedure that starts with drilling down to six or seven thousand feet beneath the sea, and ends with the production of the thousand million cubic feet of gas per day that will eventually be available.

Then the Princess was out in the open, tramping along an intricacy of narrow cat-walks and stairways, all constructed from an openwork of slippery metal poised a hundred or so feet above the dappled, cold-looking and only too apparent sea. As she crossed the area where pipes for the nearby well are loaded, a fishing smack, dressed overall, slipped inside the five-hundred yard safety limit to anchor for a grandstand view. Up beside the Kelly, a vast screw that spins the pipes down into the wells, and so called because it whirls first one way and then the other like an Irishman turning round, the Princess handled the brake controlling this enormous, complex machine, towering high into the air above her and biting deep into the rocks below the sea-bed.

Later the Princess made an unscheduled scramble

into one of the emergency Survival Capsules—
unsinkable bathoscope-like spheres, large enough
to take the entire crew; tramped up and down
to all the various levels of the rig to inspect and
be interested in everything from the cellar deck
with its well-heads to the immaculate kitchen;
and ended up with a prolonged and obviously
enjoyable lunch in the small mess room where
she also received the imaginative memento of a
plaque, with her own profile carved in com-
pressed salt drilled up from 5,600 feet below the
sea-bed.

The next day Princess Anne flew out to Germany
to pay a friendly, relatively informal visit to her

own Regiment. When the public announcement
on 10 June confirmed the Queen's appointment
of her daughter as Colonel-in-Chief of the
14/20th King's Hussars, a national newspaper
phoned the Regiment at their barracks in
Paderborn, on the edge of the Ruhr, and asked
for a comment. There were no officers available
at the time but the Staff-Sergeant epitomized the
Regiment's sentiments. 'She's a smashing girl!' he
said. 'It's the best news we've had for years!'

It was not only the officers and men who were
delighted at the thought of their new Colonel-in-
Chief, the Princess herself felt it a tremendous
honour to be asked—and what girl of nineteen
could fail to be proud and thrilled at having such
a chance!

Accompanied by the Colonel of the Regiment,
Colonel B. B. N. Woodd, M.A., Princess Anne
flew to Gütersloh, where she was welcomed by
the Station Commander of the Royal Air Force,
and by Lieut-Colonel J. M. Palmer, Commanding
Officer of her Regiment. A journey by car brought
the Princess to a civic welcome at the Rathaus
in Paderborn, where an over-enthusiastic reception by the German crowd gave her a first
acquaintance with being mobbed, and where she
pleased her German hosts by replying to the
Mayor's speech in his own language.

The Princess and Lady Susan Hussey, her Lady-
in-Waiting, were staying with Colonel Palmer
and his wife in a small, convenient house in the
married quarters provided at Barker Barracks.
That same evening Princess Anne met her
officers and their wives, before adjourning for a
splendid buffet dinner in Mess.

The dining-room that night provided a colourful,
romantic setting, the ladies in long dresses, the
officers in dark blue and scarlet mess kit with
jingling spurs; lengthy side-tables laden with
every type of delicacy the Army cooks could
devise; and the entire scene revolving round this
attractive young girl, her hair caught back with a
big black bow in the nape of her neck, the
diamanté trimming that relieved the simplicity

of her long white dress sparkling in the candle-light.

Later, accompanied by half a dozen officers and their wives, Princess Anne moved on to the friendly atmosphere of the Warrant Officers' and Sergeants' Mess to attend a ball. The Princess met, talked to and danced with as many as she could until the small hours, jiving or waltzing with equal zest to the rhythms of the regimental dance-band and an imported Italian sextet.

It rained that night, and early the next morning. And when the Regiment, under the command of the Adjutant, had been marched by squadrons onto the parade-ground to wheel, to halt and

stand at ease facing the saluting base, the reflections of the troops in their red hats and immaculate service dress were mirrored in the deep puddles. Then a breeze sprang up to chase the clouds away and the spectators furled a colourful forest of umbrellas.

The squadrons spring to attention; the Second in Command takes over, marching out with the Squadron Leaders bearing drawn swords, and the Parade is in turn taken over by the Commanding Officer; the Guidon—the Colour, to all but the Cavalry—is marched on, and two escort orderlies, resplendent in regimental full dress with busbies and white plumes, take up

position astride their borrowed horses. Tension mounts, the Press begin to stir, the parade is brought to attention. Then a Ferret Scout Car appears, preceding the entourage. The royal car stops, Princess Anne alights, the strains of the National Anthem roll out to accompany the Royal Salute—and there is a moment of light relief when Her Royal Highness's Personal Standard flutters down the flagstaff to strike terror into the heart of an escort horse.

There is a concerted rush by press photographers only just contained by a rope, as the Princess, a trim youthful figure in her white fitted coat and dashing red-and-white trilby hat, is presented with a magnificent diamond regimental brooch voluntarily subscribed for by all ranks, past and present, from all corners of the world.

The Princess pins the brooch to her lapel, and

steps out to the lilting rhythms of *Les Huguenots*, 'Boom Bang a Bang', and the appropriate 'Music to Watch Girls By', to review her Regiment.

Back at the Saluting Base she addresses the Parade, shortly and to the point, and stands there, a very young and charming Colonel-in-Chief, for the Regimental March Past, the Advance in Review Order, the Royal Salute and the cheers that conclude Princess Anne's first Parade.

Later, after a visit to Regimental Headquarters, it was the turn of the ladies—when the Princess met the soldiers' wives in the informal surroundings of the W.R.V.S. Room and drank a welcome cup of coffee with them.

The children were not forgotten. There was an interlude for an official regimental photograph, the Colonel-in-Chief seated amongst her officers and other ranks, and then she was off to the

British Forces Educational School. A visit to the bright class-rooms, a wavering treble chorus of greeting at each one; an introduction to the school guinea-pig; an amused glance for the small girl who had lost control of her skirt straps and had her arms pinioned to her sides; and a 'Well now, you're doing a lot of work, aren't you?' for the little boy, supposed to be the soul of industry, who was leaning happily on a totally empty desk.

That afternoon Princess Anne demonstrated the family aptitude for controlling machines when she spent several blissful and absorbing hours up at the Goldrund Training Area, at a display of the regiment's armoured vehicles.

Wearing khaki overalls complete with name and rank, the Princess first took off with a 432 armoured personnel carrier. She drove a Stalwart, one of the load-carrying six-wheeled amphibious vehicles that were seen in the television series *The Trouble-shooters*, before clambering up into a 50-ton Chieftain Tank, called the 'Princess Anne'. After a short briefing by a Guidon Sergeant, the Princess first traversed the turret with its 120 mm. gun, then donned earphones, and with justifiable pride became the first girl to control the most powerful mark of tank in the world, over three miles across country, and then set a new speed record for Chieftains when driving the tank herself on the return trip. On arrival back at barracks the Princess emerged from the driving seat covered in mud. 'I'd love one for Christmas!' she said.

That night Princess Anne, dining in Mess with her officers, drank, amongst other toasts, a special one to 'The Emperor', and was initiated into one of those strange traditions that colour life in the Services. A tradition that, in this case, concerns the King's Hussars' capture of the silver chamber-pot of the King of Spain, Napoleon's brother Joseph.

The next day, after touring the Regiment's lines and proving herself an expert shot with a Sterling sub-machine-gun, Princess Anne took off for Gütersloh en route for Stuttgart, the helicopter of the Queen's Flight lifting off the regimental football pitch to the strains of 'Oh, You Beautiful Doll!'

Now the Princess has another reminder of her first unforgettable visit to her Regiment. Back in England she found the gift of new number plates on her car—1420 H—that the 14/20th Hussars had managed to discover and which had previously adorned a United Dairies' milk float.

JUST BEFORE SHE WENT TO GERMANY IN October 1969, Princess Anne crowded seventeen public functions into a fortnight. Those fourteen days were exceptional, but even so it might seem that her Diary of Engagements is filling up so rapidly that, apart from riding, there is scarcely time for any private life at all.

Fortunately this is not the case, and the Princess also manages to pack a lot of unofficial fun into her busy existence, with room occasionally for one of the things she says she most enjoys . . . 'Doing nothing!'

If she is 'on duty' for the rest of the day, in London or at Windsor, Princess Anne often gets up at an hour when many people are still asleep, and slips off to Mrs Oliver's stables to school the horses. Otherwise she and Prince Charles always join their youngest brother Edward and Miss Anderson for eight o'clock breakfast in the nursery, with Prince Andrew there as well during the holidays.

The Royal Family are very united and happy in each other's company, and they are together for most of the time when at their country homes. At Buckingham Palace the Princess either lunches with the Queen and the Duke or, if she is alone, once more makes for the nursery. Sometimes she entertains her friends to a snack or a meal in her own quarters. The sitting-room she shares with Prince Charles, with its comfortable sofa and easy chairs, and the attractive inlaid mahogany furniture that came from Osborne—the former royal residence in the Isle of Wight that Queen Victoria bought in 1845 and loved dearly for the remaining fifty-six years of her life.

Now that she is very much a public figure, Princess Anne has to spend some time most morn-ings going through the ever-increasing volume of correspondence with her Lady-in-Waiting. Perched on the arm of a chair, her hair loose on her shoulders, and usually wearing the slacks or jeans she still favours for home life, the Princess decides, amongst other questions, which matters she must really deal with personally—since, like the majority of her age-group, the actual chore of settling down to write letters does not come easily.

Sometimes the Princess makes unannounced, informal visits to events that interest her. She popped in quite casually to the Ideal Home Exhibition of 1968, and to one afternoon of the Horse of the Year Show in 1969. On 28 June of that year she joined a group of young people flying out to Paris from Heathrow by a scheduled B.E.A. service flight, to a dance given by the British Ambassador, Mr Christopher Soames, and his wife, for their children Nicholas and Emma, two childhood friends of about Princess Anne's own age. She spends weekends staying with friends in the country, and often drives herself to the private dinner and cocktail parties she goes to in London.

On any day that she can do so the Princess fits in riding of some sort, either serious work with her Event horses or a dash to Windsor to hack Jinks in the park.

As with most people there are many sides to Princess Anne's personality. But perhaps the truest and most constant is the one that emerges when the Princess is living in the environment she loves—the royal country homes where jeans and a gamin cap, or a mini-kilt with hair flying free, are the order of the day.

King George V and his son King George VI,

Princess Anne's grandfather, both had a special affection for Sandringham House, the country seat on a Norfolk estate near the Wash that was bought in 1870 by Edward VII when Prince of Wales and is now one of the Queen's private homes.

The Princess, a creature of habit, always associates this home with Christmas, even though, owing to lack of room, the Royal Family now go there after the festival, spending Christmas itself at Windsor. There, at the Castle, she has a bedroom and her own sitting-room at the top of the tower allocated to her and Prince Charles, but at Sandringham she has only 'a tiny little room which looks like a dressing-room with a bed in it, and has more cupboards than anything else'. A room that is as warm and cosy as Sandringham itself.

This house is very much a home, a place where father and son leave their shooting shoes in the hall, a place that is an open invitation to play charades and hide-and-seek and other Christmassy games during the long, dark evenings.

In the grounds there are wide, inviting rides cut through the tall avenues of trees, and surrounding acres of stubble good for galloping, for those who prefer riding to shooting. When the Royal Family are in residence, the stabling accommodates some of the favourite hacks and ponies, in addition to the brood mares and young stock, which are all housed beneath the shadow of the huge, bronze statue of Persimmon—Edward VII's legendary racehorse.

At Balmoral Princess Anne also has a tiny bedroom, although it contains a rickety desk to offset the lack of a sitting-room—an amenity that would be unthinkable in the family, almost 'country cottage' atmosphere of this relatively small castle.

In her *Journal of Our Life in the Scottish Highlands*, Queen Victoria wrote of Balmoral that 'the view from the windows of our room . . . of the valley of the Dee, with the mountains in the background . . . is quite beautiful', a description that is still valid today.

For all her layers of petticoats and voluminous skirts and, by modern standards, narrow outlook, Queen Victoria had much of the independence of spirit and love of personal freedom that is inherent in her great-great-great-grand-daughter. Even so, the old Queen would not have wished even to imagine the liberty and informality that pervades Balmoral today—and which has always made the Royal Family look on the weeks in Scotland, between early August and late October, as the best in the whole year.

How do the days go? All day, every day is spent out of doors, and for Princess Anne there is first perhaps a wander round the stables—with Jinks following hard on her heels as she has taught him—to inspect the children's ponies and the sturdy Haflingers, cream mountain ponies from Austria that were presented to the Queen. Unlike her mother, walking does not appeal to

the Princess, but she gets over that problem by using a bicycle for the five hundred yards between the house and the stables, and by riding Jinks all over the estate and up wooded bridle paths to the surrounding hills, sometimes in company with the Queen or Princess Margaret. Often there is a day's shooting out on the moors, with the special interest of watching her own gun-dog at work. This is Snipe, the young daughter of the Queen's black labrador Wren, who has succeeded the old, somewhat wild yellow labrador that Princess Anne was given when she was ten.

Most days there is time to give Snipe some extra practice with dummy and whistle; and there is always time for the hazardous, laughter-filled treks between stable and field when the Princess rides Jinks bareback in a headcollar, and leads three of the other ponies with him. In the evenings the Go-Karts often emerge. Prince Andrew and Lord Linley, both wearing most necessary crash-helmets, race each other up and down the criss-crossing paths that lead to the stables, or bank perilously around the lawns. Prince Edward comes shooting out of the tower door to join the fun, and Princess Anne flashes by, Princess Margaret's small daughter, Lady Sarah, sitting between her knees, to practise her speciality—skid turns at speed on the drive, that envelop them both in clouds of dust.

All the royal children go to some of the local functions, and when they were younger Princess Anne used to help Prince Charles with a stall at Sales of Work at Crathie, where the whole family worship in the little country church each Sunday. The well-known Braemar Gathering for the Highland Games—with exhibitions of nimble-footed sword-dancing and kilted strong men tossing the caber—has also for many years been a Royal Family occasion.

Few days pass without a family picnic. Two Land Rovers are drawn up before the main door, and in a few minutes the Family, the guests, hordes of children, the corgis and picnic baskets are all packed in. Prince Charles jumps into the driving seat of the first vehicle, the Queen into that of the second, and they are off.

A moment's stop by the paddock to greet the horses and ponies, and the cars swoop out of the grounds and up on to the hill. The narrow track snakes between purple heather, grey boulders and yellowy-green bog, all chequered by the cloud shadows that sweep across the moors. The Land Rovers speed bumping over the ruts, twisting and turning up and down and around, with choking dust thrown up behind and dark hills brooding on the skyline, to come at last to a grove of tall trees, and beyond them to a small grey house standing in a clearing beside a loch.

This is Loch Muick, a lovely spot as dear to Queen Victoria as to our own Royal Family. She built the house on someone else's spit of land—which had eventually to be paid for by Princess Anne's grandfather! Here she used to come, driving up from Balmoral with horses and carriages, bringing much of her extensive household, along a track that even today, in a much better state of repair, takes twenty minutes by car. And when that intrepid Royal Lady's carriage capsized into a ditch, the laconic entry in her diary read: 'We had only a little claret with which to mop up the blood.'

The loch is very deep, with a craggy mountain on the far side that goes straight down into the water, and when the sun shines the ripples run across the surface like diamonds. On the house side there is scree at the loch edge, then green grass, and to one side a battalion of Scotch firs that have marched almost to the house wall. Left to itself the only sounds at Loch Muick are the wind in the trees, bird song, and the subdued rush of waterfalls.

The cars stop. Guests help Prince Charles with the hampers, the Queen gives Prince Andrew a hand with his aluminium boat at the water's edge, Prince Philip inspects the ingredients for the day's dish, David Linley eggs on a corgi hunting rabbits in a rhododendron bush, and Prince Edward and Lady Sarah don special

The pictures of Princess Anne and the Royal Family which appear in this chapter were taken by special permission at Balmoral, September 1969

(on them outsize) gloves, to aid Princess Anne with the first essential—coaxing charcoal to a good glow on the barbecue she has brought out from the house.

The Duke comes over to help his daughter with the fire, and then to start up the cooking. Often the Queen strolls inside the little house to inspect the state of the wallpapers and curtains that are renewed through the years in the same pattern, or to try out the recently mended musical-box with the tinkly tunes that was Queen Victoria's.

Then Prince Charles calls to his mother, and the Queen emerges to give the finishing touches to the salad he has been preparing, the children are summoned, the dogs shooed off and another picnic is under way.

84

In 1969, for the first time, Princess Anne cut short her holiday in Scotland to return south for some intensive riding and Eventing, and to compete with Royal Ocean in the Spiller's Combined Competition—comprising dressage and jumping—at the Horse of the Year Show at Wembley on 10 October. During this time she was based at the Palace, which enabled her to organize her autumn wardrobe.

When she was shopping only a year or so back someone might turn round and exclaim, 'Oh, doesn't that girl look like Princess Anne!' But now, with all the publicity surrounding her and Prince Charles, it is almost impossible not to be recognized. It has become 'just a part of life' that people should stop and stare, and she is also unworried by legitimate photography, although she 'feels stupid, when they go on doing it . . .' to excess on public occasions.

Although someone is sure to recognize her, the Princess does contrive to get about quite frequently in the evening, to the theatre or cinema, or to the occasional discothèque or night club, without her presence being reported in the Press. She never goes out with less than three other companions, but this is not only on her own account.

Publicity is an accepted and understood part of being born royal, but the Princess feels genuinely worried on account of the other people who may get involved, many of whom have little or no connexion with this aspect of her life. The acquaintances kind enough to say 'Would you like to come?' may then be exposed to the attentions of the Press, or become subjects of speculation in the daily papers. Princess Anne feels this is one of the difficulties of her position, and considers carefully before accepting any invitation. Nothing may happen, but it is always a risk and can be an embarrassing one.

The Princess's opportunities for meeting people often and getting to know them well are limited, so that first impressions are important. She is a girl of her generation and although most of the young men she counts as friends wear their hair at collar length, she does not object too strongly to the lion's-mane coiffeur some of the young affect. She 'thinks it unfortunate that appearances often deceive one', but 'if you can try to forget it, it isn't too bad!' She laughs, in the same breath, about the pot calling the kettle black . . .

The innate quality most important to Princess Anne is a sense of humour. Someone who makes her laugh has instant appeal, and these are usually the people with whom she finds a common wavelength of interest. She is suspicious of any sign of adulation, dislikes gush in any form, and looks for those who are as honest and straightforward as herself. Where she is amongst known friends at a private party she likes to be treated as an equal, but can successfully squash the too-brash new acquaintance who is stupidly familiar. She finds it difficult to bring people out of their shell, and for this reason sometimes overlooks the genuine characters, too shy and diffident to make their presence felt, in favour of those who make it easy by meeting her halfway.

One day Princess Anne is going to fall in love, one day she is going to marry—both events that appear at the moment to be of more burning interest to the public at large than to the one chiefly concerned.

It would be hard to make the Princess do anything of importance she did not wish to, let alone marry a man she did not love just because he was suitable—and with parents like the Queen and Prince Philip, this is something that is most unlikely to occur. Obviously, like any girl, Princess Anne does give thought to these matters, but rightly contends that 'You never know the answer until it happens . . .'

She acknowledges that one *can* fall head over heels in love more or less on sight, but considers that, too, a contingency to cope with if and when it occurs—and it might present no problem anyway. Having a rational mind, and being used to facing up to the drawbacks as well as the advantages of her position, the Princess hopes that if she became attached to someone who would find it too difficult to fit into her kind of existence she would be able to extricate herself before things had reached a serious stage. This is again not so

much on her own account but because, although it is easy and enjoyable for her to move in other circles, it is more difficult for someone totally unacquainted with the very considerable constrictions and conventions of royal life to move into hers—and this sense of unfairness to the man concerned would, she trusts, act as a brake in time. Young as she is, the Princess is also wise enough to realize that it is the small irritations of a different background and way of life that can so easily mar a marriage.

Princess Anne likes to consider, and discuss, the problems of the so-called permissive society and her own generation. Herself a lover of liberty, her strong views yet include a conviction that licence in sex does not produce freedom, and that too much preoccupation with a part of life that is not only important but should be private to the individual merely cheapens it. Nor can she see that freedom of speech is a possibility if only one section of society, the younger generation, is allowed to express its views. On the other hand, the Princess sympathizes with many of the protests made against world evils, and admires those who try to do something about them. But she has little time for the noisy, self-styled intellectuals who are in fact mere layabouts, and thinks it a pity they should command the publicity

that by rights belongs to the vast majority of the young people of today. The backbone of her generation, they are quietly getting on with their jobs in the world, always ready to help the old and the young, and, what is more exceptional, those of their own age-group who are in need.

Princess Anne thinks the experience of meeting other nationalities and seeing how they live is one of the most necessary and absorbing aspects of life, and she is determined to travel.

She went to Malta, Tobruk and Gibraltar when she was four, and to Germany in 1963, 1964, and again in October 1969. She had a short stay in Athens when she was bridesmaid at the Greek Royal Wedding, has been to Paris, to Liechtenstein twice, to France three times and to Switzerland once. The Princess joined Prince Charles, on his way home from Australia, in Jamaica for the Commonwealth Games in 1966, accompanied her parents to Austria and Norway in 1969, and spent a holiday in Malta with her brother directly after the Prince of Wales's Investiture.

Maybe Princess Anne wishes in her heart she could go off, as Prince Charles did to Australia, and stay informally in other countries, which would enable her to dig down beneath the surface in a way that is impossible on a formal tour. On her future travels she may find some of the answers she is seeking from life, but in the meantime, in the year since she first became a public personage in her own right, the Princess has already found some guide-lines.

On 2 June 1969 she went to open the Black-friars Youth Centre in South London. Before the formal part of the proceedings began, the Princess paid a brief visit to the Old People's Club, and then she and Lady Susan Hussey, entirely on their own except for a Senior Social Worker, spent some time with the Mother's Group called 'The Sixpenny Club'. These are women from a slum district behind the Old Vic, who have been housed with their families in 'temporary' transition apartments to await other accommodation. Some of them have been

waiting for seven or eight years, and most of them have given up hope. The Settlement does a wonderful job in giving an eye to the children and providing them with square meals at intervals, besides running the Club as the one bright spot in the week. But these are women who no longer have the desire, or ability, to keep themselves or their homes clean, and can no longer cope with their problems. The majority of their husbands are out of work, many are in prison, and the look of utter despair in those women's eyes was not just something that Princess Anne had never met before—it was unbelievable to her that such misery and poverty could exist in a country such as England.

That afternoon they had smartened themselves up for the Princess's benefit, but were at first shy and tongue-tied until her genuine sympathy and warmth gradually took effect. Then they sat beside her and opened their hearts, telling her of problems that they had possibly never voiced before, and of a kind she had never thought of. It was the old-faced girl beside her, already a mother of two children, who struck the deepest note. 'I'm the same age as you, Princess Anne', she said. 'I was born six hours before you . . .'

There was one way in which the Princess was able to give them pleasure. She discovered that they often brought their children to see the Changing of the Guard, but could never get through the crowd, and she was able to promise that all the children from the Settlement could come together, and stand inside the Palace gates for a front-line view. But apart from this, it was the first time Princess Anne realized that it can help just to listen, and she decided there and then that, if this was one way she could assist people, just by acting as a safety-valve, then that should be part of her job in life.

Another part would seem to lie with children.

The affinity children seem to feel with her is something Princess Anne finds inexplicable. She says—not entirely seriously—of her own young brothers, that Edward gets on her nerves,

possibly because he is said to be very like her at that age, and that with Andrew she can just about survive the holidays before he drives her quite up the wall!

She refuses to take Andrew riding, because, she says, 'It's instant death—he always falls off with me!' But she did have Edward as passenger when she drove the Haflingers as a pair at a meet of the Driving Society on Smith's Lawn in June 1969, and was placed in the Concours d'Élégance class. The Princess stands no nonsense with either of her young brothers, yet those in the know consider she is remarkably good with, and for them—and they, like other children, think she is 'the tops'.

Children do like being treated as equals, and, like animals, hate to be fussed over. They trust those who do not make obvious advances, and have an unerring instinct for what lies at the heart of a person. Once when the Princess and her young cousin David Linley were bicycling around the paths at Balmoral, as usual at speed and in this instance in opposite directions, they collided forcibly on one of the corners. The Princess was not entirely undamaged but the small boy, and his bicycle, came off worse. In a

moment she had picked him up, and in the gentlest, most endearing manner was urging him to count his toes and fingers, assuring him his nose was in one piece and that he still possessed a couple of eyes—and in no time had turned his tears to laughter.

Partly because she cannot understand why it should be so, it flatters Princess Anne that children do like her, and since it seems good sense to do what one appears to be good at, she says, 'Well, if children are going to like me for some reason, then let me be involved with children . . .'

Between March 1969, when she began her public life, and November that same year, the Princess attended thirteen public functions actively connected with young people. Those specifically concerning children ranged from the riding class for Spastic Children she watched during her visit to the National Equestrian Centre on 25 April to receiving purses on behalf of the Church of England Children's Society at the Royal Albert Hall on 22 October. Then on 25 November it was announced that Princess Anne had agreed to succeed Lord Boyd of Merton as President of the Save the Children Fund—the first appointment of this kind that she had taken on.

Whatever Princess Anne eventually decides to do, she will do it wholeheartedly, and choose something in which she can become totally involved. In the meantime she is fulfilling part of her mission in life, in a position that consciously or unconsciously does affect a great many people, simply by being the sort of girl she is.

The Princess is trying to learn that requirement of royalty, to 'tread warily'. She has become accustomed to that strange constraint, liable to descend suddenly and for no apparent reason in the presence of royalty, such as the bunch of children with whom, at the age of thirteen, she had been chattering happily and riding around Windsor Park—only to have them, at the mere sight of the Queen offering biscuits all round in the stable yard, become so paralysed with shyness that they could neither eat nor say 'No, thank you!'

She remains as independent as ever. Even though the Princess has now acquired the sole services of Miss Gardner to look after her clothes the job entails none of the duties of an old-time 'lady's maid'. Her possessions remain as unpretentious as when she first left school. Even her beloved car has only four extra gadgets—a 'tape' attached to the radio for her cassettes, a rev counter, a heated rear window, and the Triplex laminated windscreen that would have saved the previous one from shattering.

The Princess looks horrified at the thought of being held up as an example, but Prince Philip puts the position in a nutshell. When asked, during an interview in America, about the role of the monarchy, the Duke suggested that amongst other assets 'it has the advantage that it involves a whole family, which means that different age-groups are part of it . . . There are people who can look, for instance, at the Queen Mother and say they identify with that generation, or with us, or with our children.'

If Princess Anne were the journalistic, sugary Princess that used to be portrayed some years back she would make little impact, one way or the other, on her own generation or on anyone else, but this girl with the strong personality is as large as life, faults and all.

She integrates with the youth of today, freedom-loving, impatient, intolerant of fools, yet sensitive to the feelings and advice of older people—and the abiding love and admiration she feels for her parents is a dominating factor in her life.

If an ice-cream carton, thrown during the drive through Caernarvon streets at the Investiture, had happened to hit, instead of just miss the Princess's hat, she would have been quite capable of jumping down and thumping the thrower. She has a temper that can inflame to shouting-point, but is quick to acknowledge when she is in the wrong. Completely honest, both to herself and others, utterly loyal to her friends, Princess Anne will always take, and act on justified criticism. She has a quick wit, a quicker, sometimes biting tongue, is gay, amusing, and loves to laugh. She has a shrewdness beyond her years, and when it comes to the point, will always put what she sees to be her duty above any private inclination.

Princess Anne has, not always of her own volition, packed a great variety of experience into her first nineteen years. Part of her life is enviable; the interesting people she meets, the fascinating things she does, all help to make her the attractive girl she is—but much of the job of being a modern Princess is a tougher task than many would care to undertake. And Princess Anne is making an admirable job of it.

HER ROYAL HIGHNESS THE PRINCESS ANNE
FOURTH IN SUCCESSION AND SECOND LADY IN THE LAND

BIRTH

Tuesday 15 August, 1950 at Clarence House. Weight 6 lb

CHRISTENING

21 October, 1950: At Buckingham Palace by the Archbishop of York

Names: Anne Elizabeth Alice Louise

Godparents: H.M. The Queen (Queen Elizabeth the Queen Mother), Princess Andrew of Greece, Princess Margarita of Hohenlohe-Langenburg, Earl Mountbatten, Hon. Andrew Elphinstone

CHURCH

1953 Christmas Day, first went to church, Sandringham

EARLY EDUCATION

1955 Autumn: regular lessons started with Miss Peebles, Prince Charles's governess

1957 May: Caroline Hamilton and Susan Babington-Smith joined Palace class and remained until Her Royal Highness went to school in September 1963

1961 October: General lessons in French, picture-study etc., two afternoons a week, with Mrs Untermeyer (a friend of the Queen)

1962 Summer Term: Extra history with Mrs Garvin
        November: Latin lessons from Mr Trevor Roberts

1962 Visit to France with Mrs Untermeyer, staying with Marquis de St Genys, to learn French

FRENCH

1957 August: French governess, Mlle Bibiane de Roujoux, at Balmoral for a month

1959 May onwards: Mlle Suzanne Josseron, several times a week to Palace class

        August: Lt Jean Lajeunesse, French-Canadian officer, at Balmoral for a month

1968 October: 6-week intensive French course at Berlitz School of Languages

BROWNIES AND GUIDES

1959 May: Palace Brownie Pack re-formed
        July: Enrolled in Pixie six

1961 May: Guide Meeting (1st Buckingham Palace Coy) held at Palace. July: Enrolled in Kingfisher patrol

1962 8-12 June: First camp in Sussex

1963 27 July-2 August: Second camp at Maldon Island

FLYING

1955 May: First flight in a helicopter at Windsor
        June: First flight in an aeroplane, Dyce (Scotland)–London Airport

AILMENTS

1958 May: Tonsils and adenoids removed at Great Ormond Street Hospital for Sick Children

1959 April: Chicken-pox—at Windsor Castle

1961 March: Whooping-cough—at Buckingham Palace
        April: Measles—at Windsor Castle

BRIDESMAID

1960 13 January: Wedding of her cousin Lady Pamela Mountbatten to Mr David Hicks at Romsey Abbey

        6 May: Chief Bridesmaid at Princess Margaret's wedding to Mr Anthony Armstrong-Jones at Westminster Abbey

1961 8 June: Wedding of the Duke of Kent and Miss Katharine Worsley at York Minster

1963 24 April: Wedding of Princess Alexandra to Mr Angus Ogilvy at Westminster Abbey

1964 18 September: Wedding of King Constantine of Greece and Princess Anne-Marie of Denmark at Athens

SCHOOL

1963 20 September-23 July 1968: Benenden School, independent boarding school, girls 12½ years upwards, about 300 pupils in all.

Headmistress: Miss E. B. Clarke, M.A., B.Litt. (Oxon), J.P. *House Mistress*: Miss C. Gee, B.A. (Bristol), M.A. (Bryn Mawr, U.S.A.) *House*: Guldeford

G.C.E. 1966 'O' Levels: Passes in English Language, English Literature (A), French, History, Geography, Biology. Failed: Latin. Also passed: Royal Society of Arts test in Arithmetic

1968 Advanced Levels: Passes in History (Grade D. Grade 2 (Merit) in special optional extra paper), Geography (Grade E)

VISITS ABROAD

1954 14 April: Embarked R.Y. *Britannia* at Portland
        22-28 April: Malta

        30 April-1 May: Tobruk (Meeting the Queen and Prince Philip on final stage of Commonwealth Tour)

1954 3-7 May: Malta. 10-11 May: Gibraltar
15 May: Returned London
1962 4-13 July: France. Private educational visit
1963 16-20 April: Germany. Visiting relations with Prince Philip
1964 14-15 September: Langen, Germany
15-20 September: Greece. Athens, Royal Wedding
29 December: France, Paris en route—
30 December-8 January 1965: Liechtenstein. Ski-ing
1965 28 December-1 January 1966: Liechtenstein. Ski-ing
1966 3-8 January: Switzerland. Ski-ing
8-9 January: Liechtenstein. Ski-ing
3-8 March: Jamaica—Commonwealth Games
1967 20-21 April: Nice—International Horse Show
1969 19-29 March: Val d'Isère, France. Ski-ing
7-10 May: Austria—accompanied the Queen and Prince Philip on State Visit
28 June: Paris—dance given by Mr and Mrs Christopher Soames
7-14 July: Malta—holiday with Prince Charles
7-12 August: Norway—Summer cruise
29-31 October: Paderborn, Germany. 14/20th King's Hussars

DRIVING
1968 17 April: Passed Driving Test at first attempt
October: Given blue Rover 2000, gift for eighteenth birthday

PORTRAITS
1949 Conversation Piece. Clarence House Drawing Room by Edward Halliday. Owned by Queen Mother
1952 Miniature, water-colour by Stella Marks, owned by the Queen
1953 Pastels by Urica Forbes, owned by the Queen and Queen Mother
1957 Sketch, head only, by A. K. Lawrence, owned by the Queen
1958 Sketch on horseback, by M. le Comte de Poret, owned by the Queen

FIRST STATE OCCASIONS ETC.
1967 31 October: State Opening of Parliament
1968 25 July: Attended a Buckingham Palace Garden Party
1969 23 April: Attended State Banquet for President Saragat of Italy—at Windsor Castle
7-10 May: State Visit to Austria

DECORATIONS AND APPOINTMENTS
1969 23 April: Family Order given by the Queen before State Banquet for President Saragat
7 May: Austrian Order of Merit
10 June: Colonel-in-Chief 14/20th King's Hussars

15 July: Grand Cross of the White Rose of Finland
November: President of the Save the Children Fund

PUBLIC FUNCTIONS IN HER OWN RIGHT
1969 1 March: Elizabeth Barracks, Pirbright—to present leeks to 1st Battalion Welsh Guards
25 April: Rover Company, Solihull. The National Equestrian Centre and opening Young Farmers' Club Centre, Kenilworth, Stoneleigh
26 April: Wembley Stadium, F.A. Cup Final
2 May: Tyneside—launching s.s. *Esso Northumbria*
22 May: Edinburgh—Dunforth House for Children
23 May: Edinburgh—R.S.S.P.C.C. Shelter
26 May: London. Lunch and opening of Festival of London Stores
2 June: London. Opening Blackfriars Youth Centre
3 June: London. World premiere film *Run Wild, Run Free*, Odeon Theatre, Leicester Square in aid of Textile Benevolent Society
25 June: Lancaster House, Garden Party for Teachers from the Commonwealth
4 July: Wimbledon, Lawn Tennis Championships
21 July: Royal Gala Performance *Alfred the Great*, Empire, Leicester Square—in aid of Scout Association
22 July: Newmarket, opening Small Animal Centre, Kennett, and visit to Equine Research Station
23 July: Private Visit, BBC TV Centre, Wood Lane, London, W.12
10 September: High Ercall to open Road Transport Industry Training Board's education centre
27 September: East Lothian. Reception in aid of Save the Children Fund, Gosford House, Longniddry
20 October: Visit to Chelmsford and Colchester
21 October: Dover. Naming second Mountbatten Class Hovercraft *The Princess Anne*
22 October: Royal Albert Hall. Receiving purses on behalf of the Church of England Children's Society
23 October: Mansion House. Luncheon by The Watch Ashore
24 October: Visit to Manchester and Bolton
25 October: Young Adventurers' Club, 145 Iverson Road, London, N.W.6. To open The Homesteader
27 October: Visit to Bristol
28 October: North Sea. AMOCO 'B' Gas Rig
29-31 October: Paderborn, Germany. Visit to 14/20th King's Hussars as Colonel-in-Chief

RIDING
1953 February: First lessons
1963-1968: Between 20 September and 23 July, instruction at Moat House, Benenden, by Mrs Hatton-Hall
1968 Spring onwards: Schooling for Eventing by Mrs Alan Oliver, at Brookfield Farm, Warfield
1969 Horse Trials and Competitions

PHOTOGRAPHS

Pages 4, 10, 12, 45 by Gracious Permission of Her Majesty the Queen
from her private family albums
Pages 41-44, 78, 80-87, 90, 91, 95 by Nicholas Flower
Page 74 by Glyn Gemin, *Financial Times*
Title-page and pages 7, 11, 14, 19, 23, 26, 30, 31, 34, 36-39, 40, 46,
50-51, 53, 54-55, 58, 61, 62-63, 65, 66, 67, 69, 70, 96 by John Scott and
Overseas Photo and Feature Agency Ltd
Page 92 by Lord Snowdon
Page 75 by Associated Press
Page 13 by Barratt's Photo Press Ltd
Pages 20, 21, 24, 25, 28 by Central Press Agency
Pages 72, 73, 76 Crown Copyright
Pages 6, 8, 64 by Fox Photos Ltd
Pages 29, 56, 68, 89 by Keystone Press Agency Ltd
Page 33 by Paul Popper Ltd

DESIGNED BY CRAIG DODD

CASSELL & COMPANY LTD
35 RED LION SQUARE, LONDON, WC1
Melbourne Sydney Toronto Johannesburg Auckland

© Judith Campbell 1970
First published 1970
I.S.B.N.   0 304 93589 1

Printed and bound in Great Britain by Bookprint Limited, Crawley, Sussex